THE

TITLES OF OUR LORD

ADOPTED BY HIMSELF

IN THE

NEW TESTAMENT.

BY

J. MONTAGU RANDALL,

VICAR OF LANGHAM, NORFOLK.

"I am the door." — JOHN X. 9.

PHILADELPHIA:

PRESBYTERIAN BOARD OF PUBLICATION,

No. 821 CHESTNUT STREET.

PREFACE.

THE circumstances under which this little work has been prepared, will, it is hoped, bespeak in its favour the indulgence of the religious public. Nearly blind, the author has been unable to consult many books, which would have afforded him important assistance. The whole has been written in pencil in a *chiragon*,* and afterwards transcribed with the greatest care. Only those who, like the author, have written consecutive paragraphs which they could not read, can realize the increase of labour occasioned by the loss of sight. As a thank-offering to his heavenly Father for unnumbered mercies, he has been anxious to cast his mite into the treasury of the Church of Christ, and he fervently prays that it may please the Lord Jesus to accompany its perusal with his effectual blessing.

LANGHAM, *September* 1858.

* An instrument used by the blind to guide the hand in writing.

CONTENTS.

THE TITLES OF OUR LORD

ADOPTED BY HIMSELF

IN THE

NEW TESTAMENT.

INTRODUCTION.

It has been computed that there are more than one hundred glorious names and titles of our blessed Lord in the Scriptures: none present so instructive and interesting a group as those which he has been pleased to assume to himself in the New Testament. We have read of an ancient city celebrated for its hundred gates: the names of Jesus Christ are like so many gates, through which we are invited to enter and contemplate the graces and the glories of his character. The city of God, the New Jerusalem, is described in the visions of John as having twelve gates, and it is added that "every several gate was of one pearl," Rev. xxi. 21. We are thus taught that our only way of acceptance with God is through Jesus Christ; that he is accessible to penitent sinners in all parts of the world; that from whatever quarter we look upon him, we behold a blessed and precious unity in his character: "every gate is of one pearl."

If we consider the names and titles which Christ has assumed to himself, we shall soon discover that the idea which pervades them all is that of relationship towards, and solicitude for, his believing people. By his Divine perfections, as our Creator, and by experimental contact, Jesus Christ knows us through and through. "He needeth not that any should testify of man: for he knows what is in man." "He knoweth our frame: he remembereth that we are dust." He is, moreover, a Saviour perfectly adapted to our necessities, the very Friend we need. And it is a proof of his grace and mercy, that when he speaks of himself, and unfolds to us his own character and attributes, he speaks to our very hearts, and assumes the very attributes and qualifications which will commend him the most to our confidence and gratitude. Is not the name of "Jesus" a balm for every wound, a cordial for our fear? Is he not the "Christ," anointed of the Father to preach the gospel to the poor? Is he not the "bread of life" for our famishing souls? Is he not the "light" of this dark, sorrow-stricken world? Is he not the "door" by which we may enter into his fold of peace, liberty, and joy? And is he not the "good Shepherd" who gave his life for his sheep? With what sympathy does he speak to the bereaved and desolate, when he calls himself "the resurrection and the life!" With what care for our real happiness does he give his own example to our imitation, and charge us to follow him as our "Lord and Master!" Where, in such few words, can we find a more complete unfolding of his character than when he says of himself, "I am the way, the truth, and the life?" Can any image set forth more vividly our dependence upon him, and the fulness of the grace in him for us, than that of the "true vine?" "We are saved by hope." Can anything be more cheering than to hear him say to us at the close of the sacred volume, "I am the bright and morning star?"

In all these titles there is nothing of self-exaltation, for the "Son of man came not to be ministered unto, but to minister" consolation and grace to his followers. Even in the august name "I Am," though he claimed the prerogatives of Jehovah, yet its simplicity and brevity are quite as striking as its majesty and mystery. And when he called himself "Alpha and Omega," it was for the comfort of his afflicted church, and to assure his suffering servants to the end of time, that as he had been the "Author," so he would also be the "Finisher of their faith."

The names of the Lord Jesus are real things, not a mere pageant or an empty sound; but what Christ calls himself that he is. Among men, titles are frequently bestowed which are undeserved; Christ has a pre-eminent right to every title assigned to him in the Bible, but no title does justice to him. He is what it implies, but *more;* more than *all combined*, yea, combined in their *best* state; and infinitely more. He is not only *perfect*, but *Divine.* Among men, names and titles are chiefly a benefit to the person who enjoys them. The titles of Christ are the glory and salvation of his redeemed. "The name of the Lord is a strong tower; the righteous runneth into it, and is safe."

Names are frequently redolent with fragrant memories. What pleasant associations did Bethel, the hill Mizar, and the river Chebar furnish to Jacob, David, and Ezekiel! How dear to recollection are the names of places where some auspicious event has occurred, some unexpected relief has been experienced, some peculiar and never-to-be-forgotten answer to prayer has been vouchsafed! With what satisfaction do our thoughts linger around the name of a revered parent, a spiritual counsellor or friend, who, though removed, yet seem to speak to us from day to day! If all this be true in regard to earthly scenes and friendships, how much more does it obtain of that "Friend who loveth at all times," and that "Brother born for adversity!" To the devout Christian, the names and titles of Christ are as "ointment poured forth;" he has "sat down under" the Redeemer's "shadow with great delight, and his fruit was sweet to his taste." As he reviews the path by which he has been led, he can point to seasons of high and holy communion, when the names of Jesus have been applied by the Holy Ghost with tranquillizing and satisfying power; and thus, "fitly spoken" to his inmost soul by the Divine Comforter, they have been like "apples of gold in pictures of silver."

May the unction of the Holy One accompany our feeble endeavour to explore the treasures of the names of Jesus, and make it effectual in promoting the consolation of his believing people.

"I AM."

"Jesus said unto them, Verily, verily, I say unto you, Before Abraham was, I am."—JOHN viii. 58.

THE clouds of a retreating storm are often fringed with the brightest light, and their silver edges look like doors opening into Paradise. "When the night is drearest, the morn is nearest." It is the glory of God to bring the greatest good out of the greatest evil, and to make the darkest sorrow to be the harbinger of the deepest joy.

Never did blasphemy put on a haughtier front than when the Jews said to the Son of the Blessed, "Thou art a Samaritan, and hast a devil;" and never were meekness and majesty more sweetly blended than in the Saviour's reply, "I have not a devil; but I honour my Father, and ye do dishonour me. And I seek not mine own glory: there is one that seeketh and judgeth. Verily, verily, I say unto you, If a man keep my saying, he shall never see death." Upon this the Jews repeat their awful blasphemy: "Now we know that thou hast a devil. Abraham is dead, and the prophets; and thou sayest, If a man keep my saying, he shall never taste of death. Art thou greater than our father Abraham, which is dead? and the prophets are dead: whom makest thou thyself? Jesus answered, If I honour myself, my honour is nothing: it is my Father that honoureth me, of whom ye say that he is your God: yet ye have not known him; but I know him: and if I should say, I know him not, I shall be a liar like unto you: but I know him, and keep his saying. Your father Abraham rejoiced to see my day: and he saw it, and was glad."

We need not pause here to inquire what was the measure of evangelical light enjoyed by the ancient patriarchs; neither can we decide what was the special occasion on which Abraham rejoiced in the prospect of the day of Christ. Was it when Melchisedec, one "like unto the Son of God," met him returning from his victorious war? Was it when he entertained the Divine stranger, who visited him with the two angels, and who gave him the promise of a son, and with whom he interceded in behalf of Sodom? Did he realize in the expulsion of the bondwoman and her son an allegory, radiant with gospel promises and gospel peace? Or was it when he was directed by the voice of God from heaven to offer the ram instead of his son, and when the promise of the blessing of the nations through his Seed was confirmed in the most solemn manner, and when he "called the name of that place Jehovah-jireh," saying, "In the mount of the Lord it shall be seen?" We do not know what was the special occasion to which Jesus referred, when he said, "Your father Abraham rejoiced to see my day: and he saw it, and was glad." But we know that the ancient believers looked forward with eager faith and hope to the advent of Christ in the flesh, even as we look back upon his advent as the one foundation for our acceptance and peace. They built their faith upon the promise of a Saviour who was yet to come; we build our faith upon the fulfilment of that promise in the Saviour who has come. Abraham rejoiced, his very heart leaped for joy and eagerness of holy desire for the day of Christ; and we are taught to look for and hasten unto the day of his glory, when "he shall appear the second time without sin unto salvation." The first advent of Jesus is the centre of our faith; and his second advent is the centre of our hope. Round these two foci of the grand ellipse, so to speak, of the Christian system, the thoughts and purposes of God, and the hopes and the destinies of man, are speeding onwards to their final realization.

"Thou art not yet fifty years old, and hast thou seen Abraham?" Such was the rejoinder of the Jews, marked by unbelief and surprise. The incarnate Saviour was only thirty-three, according to the years of his humiliation in the flesh; but care and sorrow, and sympathy for man, had furrowed his features with the lineaments of age: "His visage was so marred more than any man, and his form more than the sons of men." Jesus said unto them, "Verily, verily, I say unto you, Before Abraham was, I am." Thus were the unbelief and blasphemy of the Jews a platform, on which Jesus manifested his own Divine glory. Never had blasphemy so awful occasioned a confession so sublime and replete with consolation and instruction.

Let us draw near with humble reverence, and contemplate the glorious title which the Lord Jesus has been pleased to assume: "Before Abraham was, I am." Not before Abraham was, I *was*, as some critics interpret it; this would only imply the pre-existence of Christ, and not necessarily his Deity. Nor is there any ground for the cold interpretation of the Socinian, who reads the passage, "Before Abraham was, I am," that is, I was appointed to be the Messiah, the Teacher and Exemplar sent from God. Here, indeed, is partial truth, but not the sublime truth of the text; for, by a striking and peculiar form of expression, Jesus claims to himself the name which God appropriated when he said to Moses, "I Am that I Am: thus shalt thou say unto the children of Israel, I Am hath sent me unto you." God had revealed himself to the patriarchs as "God Almighty," but by his name Jehovah he was not generally known to them. Now he assumed a name even more significant and comprehensive than Jehovah, "I Am that I Am." And when the Lord Jesus claimed this title, nothing could be more clear than that, in so doing, he claimed all the prerogatives and attributes of Deity.

"I Am." This title teaches us the self-existence of Christ. The creature is a dependent being; God alone is independent and self-existent. *We* depend more or less upon each other. "The king himself is served by the field." No man, except in pride and arrogance, can say, "I am." Only the Great First Cause of all has a right to say, "I am God, and there is none else." Marvellous indeed are the manifestations of his almighty power. If on some winter's night we lift up our eyes, and "consider the heavens, the moon and the stars, which he has ordained," the number, distance, and magnitude of those magnificent orbs; and the conclusion—apparently so irresistible—from analogy, and from the benevolence and wisdom of God, that these worlds are all inhabited by intelligent creatures who exalt their Maker's praise; if from this high study we turn our attention to our own tiny ball, and reflect upon the countless tenants of earth, and air, and sea; and then meditate upon our own mental and physical constitution, we shall form some poor and inadequate idea of the self-existence and power of God, and we shall exclaim with the psalmist, "Great is our Lord, and of great power: his understanding is infinite."

When Jesus said, "Before Abraham was, I am," he claimed the Divine attribute of self-existence. All power is his in heaven and earth. "By him all things were created." "In him was life." In perfect harmony with these testimonies, we find that in the performance of his miracles, he exercised supreme, almighty, and independent power. To the suppliant leper he said, "I will, be thou clean;" and the leprosy, curable by God alone, was immediately cleansed. Under his feet the surging billows of the sea of Galilee became a solid pavement, on which he walked to the relief of his terrified disciples. Three instances are recorded of Jesus raising the dead: an only son, an only daughter, and an only brother. In all of these Christ spoke with authority as the great "I Am." "Young man, I say unto thee, Arise." "Talitha cumi." "Lazarus, come forth." His own resurrection was in his own power. "No man taketh my life from me, but I lay it down of myself. I have power to lay it down, and I have power to take it again." How consoling is the thought of Christ's almighty power! Jesus, the great "I Am," is able to save to the uttermost all that come to God by him. "He is able to keep that which we have committed unto him against that day." "Is anything too hard for the Lord?" Art thou harassed by temptation, oppressed with trials, besieged by spiritual enemies? Rest upon his word; comfort and encourage yourself in him. "Fear not, thou worm Jacob, I will help thee." "Thou art small," but "thou shalt thresh the mountains," yea, thou shalt be more than conqueror through Him who has loved thee.

This glorious name implies the unchangeableness of God, "I Am that I Am." Change is written upon everything earthly. The flower, the fruit, the grass wither and perish. Man himself "continueth not in one stay." The infant, the child, the youth, the man, the grave, all remind us of our changing condition. But our God is immutable. "I am the Lord, I change not; therefore ye sons of Jacob are not consumed." "The Strength of Israel will not lie, nor repent: for he is not a man, that he should repent." Place a cube where and how you will, and it will always present the same front. Analyse a portion of air from the summit of Mont Blanc, or from one of the crowded lanes of London, and it always contains the same proportion of its primary elements. Our God is ever the same. The billows of a thousand generations may sweep over the rock, but the rock is steadfast. "God is our Rock, his work is perfect;" "From everlasting to everlasting he is God;" his purpose and counsel shall stand, and the thoughts of his heart from generation to generation.

Jesus Christ is an unchangeable Saviour. He calls himself "I Am." He is "the same yesterday, and to-day, and for ever." Mark the quotation which Paul makes from Psalm ci. 24, 25, in the first chapter of the Epistle to the Hebrews, "To the Son he saith, Thou, Lord, in the beginning hast laid the foundation of the earth; and the heavens are the works of thine hands: they shall perish; but thou remainest; and they all shall wax old as doth a garment; and as a vesture shalt thou fold them up, and they shall be changed: but thou art the same, and thy years shall not fail." The love of God is an everlasting love. "Yea, I have loved thee with an everlasting love: therefore with loving-kindness have I drawn thee;" and those whom Jesus loves, he loves unto the end. His "sheep shall never perish," neither shall any one pluck them out of his hand. "Can a woman forget her sucking child, that she should not have compassion on the son of her womb? Yea, they may forget, yet will I not forget thee." The names of his penitent and believing people are inscribed upon his heart, and, like the jewels in the ephod, are presented by him before his Father with an everlasting remembrance.

There is, moreover, implied in this name the unfathomable mystery of God's being and character. "I Am that I Am." "Canst thou by searching find out God? Canst thou find out the Almighty to perfection? It is as high as heaven; what canst thou do? deeper than hell; what canst thou know?" In the 77th Psalm we read two remarkable statements; in the 19th verse, "Thy way is in the sea, and thy path in the great waters, and thy footsteps are not known." There is a depth in the dispensations of God, and specially with his own children, which eternity alone can disclose. But in his mercy, he has not left us altogether without a clue: "Thy way, O God, is in the sanctuary," we read in the 13th verse: "who is so great a God as our God?" Yes, Christian, in thine hours of sorrow, wait upon the Lord in the sanctuary, honour him in his own appointed ordinance; and when thou hast fully and unreservedly opened thy heart to thy Father, he may be pleased to cast a ray of his sunshine into thy soul, and to open a little of his dealings with thee; he will reveal to thee as much as thou canst receive here, and more than enough to cover thine unbelief with shame, and to humble thee before him in the deepest confidence, adoration, and love. It was so with Asaph: his perplexity was the prosperity of the wicked. How was this problem solved? When he "went into the sanctuary of God, then understood he their end." And has not many a child of God echoed the language of Asaph from the depth of his heart? "So foolish was I, and ignorant: I was as a beast before thee. Nevertheless I am continually with thee: thou hast holden me by my right hand. Thou shalt guide me with thy counsel, and afterward receive me to glory. Whom have I in heaven but thee?

and there is none upon earth that I desire beside thee. My flesh and my heart faileth: but God is the strength of my heart, and my portion for ever." Even in the day of his humiliation, there was frequently deep mystery in the dispensations of Christ. With what apparent roughness and severity did he exercise the woman of Canaan! How mysterious, for a little season, were his dealings with the woman of Samaria! How strange to the two sisters must his delay of two days have appeared! "Jesus loved Martha, and her sister, and Lazarus. When he heard therefore that he was sick, he abode two days still in the same place where he was." "But wisdom is justified of her children." And however mysterious the ways of Christ may for a time appear, we shall acknowledge that we have been led by the right way, and that all the paths of the Lord are mercy and truth, and "that not one thing hath failed of the good things which the Lord our God hath spoken; all are come to pass, not one thing hath failed thereof."

All-sufficiency is also implied in this glorious name, "I Am that I Am." That great Being, who is self-existent in himself, is all-sufficient for us. To teach this, he simply says, "I am." Bishop Beveridge makes a fine remark on this part of our subject:—"When the Lord speaks of himself with regard to his creatures, and especially his people, he calls himself 'Jehovah—I Am that I Am,' Ex. iii. 14. We should understand this of God the Father, and of God the Son, and of God the Holy Ghost, one God. He does not say, I am their light, their life, their tower, their strength; but only 'I am.' He sets his hand, as it were, to a blank, that his people may write under it what they please, that is for their good. As if he should say, 'Are they weak?—*I am* strength. Are they sick?—*I am* health. Are they in trouble?—*I am* comfort. Are they poor?—*I am* riches. Are they dying?—*I am* life. Have they nothing?—*I am* all things. *I am* justice and mercy. *I am* grace and goodness. *I am* glory, beauty, holiness, eminency, supremacy, perfection, all-sufficiency, eternity—Jehovah. *I am* whatsoever is suitable to their nature, or convenient for them in their several conditions. *I am* whatsoever is amiable in itself, or desirable to their souls. Whatever is pure and holy, whatever is great and pleasant, whatever is good, and needful to make them happy, that *I am*." So that, in short, God here represents himself unto us as one universal good;. and leaves us to make the application to ourselves, according to our several wants, capacities, and desires; he saying, only in the general—"I am."

To the pious Israelite this name would speak volumes of consolation. Was Pharaoh a haughty and imperious monarch, whose will was law, and whose frown was death? Had he at his bidding innumerable hordes of soldiers; and were the Israelites a nation of slaves, whose spirit was crushed and broken by grievous bondage? Still the God of the Hebrews was the great "I Am," of infinite and almighty power to subdue their proud tyrants, and to bring them out with a mighty hand and a stretched-out arm into a "land flowing with milk and honey." God had been pleased to enter into covenant with their fathers, with Abraham, Isaac, and Jacob, and his name assured them that he was unchangeably faithful to his covenant engagement, and would perform his promise and his oath to a thousand generations. Did it frequently appear to them a hopeless, an almost impossible matter that they should be delivered from their galling bondage? could they suggest no plan for a safe and successful departure from Egypt? What then? their God was "I Am that I Am." His understanding was infinite: what was hard and intricate to man, was easy and simple to God; all events were under his control; all means at the disposal of his perfect and unerring wisdom. The Israelites might therefore trust and not be afraid; the great "I Am" was with them, and liberty and prosperity welcomed them forward.

Let Christians rejoice in their adorable Saviour. He is the "Mighty God," of unchangeable love and exhaustless resources of wisdom and grace. Your enemies, O ye humble followers of the Lamb, may be subtle, powerful, and malicious. Satan and his legions, the world and its opposing seductions, the traitor within and your remaining corruptions, may all unite to obstruct your progress. But "rejoice in the Lord," rejoice in the almighty power of your blessed Redeemer, rejoice and fear not, for "greater is He that is with you, than all they who are against you." He has ever linked your cause with his own by a "covenant, ordered in all things and sure." He has given unto you "precious promises," suited to your every need in the wilderness, and his word cannot be broken; his counsel shall stand; his covenant shall be graciously accomplished in the complete and final salvation of all his true people. Your path may be rough and thorny: it was even so with him, the "Man of sorrows;" your path may be hedged up; mountains of difficulty, seas of opposition, and hosts of enemies may encompass you, and threaten your destruction; but your "Redeemer is mighty," and his wisdom is infinite. He loves to surprise his people. The deeper your troubles, the darker your prospects, the more formidable your enemies, the more entirely your way appears to be shut up, the more there seems to be a sentence of death written upon every means of escape, the more triumphantly and unexpectedly will He appear for your relief and succour.

Banish, then, every fear to the winds. Put the whole trust of your mind and heart in Jesus, the great "I am." Wait upon him, honour him, love him, obey him. "At evening time it shall be light." "He turneth the shadow of death into the morning."

"ALPHA AND OMEGA."

"I am Alpha and Omega, the beginning and the ending, saith the Lord, which is, and which was, and which is to come, the Almighty."—REV. i. 8.

"ALPHA" is the first letter, and "Omega" the last letter in the Greek alphabet. By uniting these two in one appellation, Jesus Christ illustrates the eternity of his Divine nature.

To escape from this proof of the Deity of Jesus, it has been said, that the words which stand at the head of this chapter are the words, not of the Son, but of the Father. The seventh verse plainly speaks of the second coming of Jesus "with clouds, when every eye shall see him." The inspired apostle —and all true believers echo his prayer — says, "Even so, Amen." "Even so, come, Lord Jesus." To assure the faithful disciple of the certainty of his coming, Jesus says, "I am Alpha and Omega, the beginning and the ending," the Creator of the world, and its final Judge. In this view, the whole connection is easy and natural; and, but for a special object, we think no one would have hazarded the opinion that the speaker of these words was God the Father. Further, there can be no question that the speaker in verse 11 is the Lord Jesus; "I am Alpha and Omega, the first and the last: and, what thou seest, write in a book, and send it unto the seven churches which are in Asia." For when John turned to see who addressed him, he beheld "one like unto the Son of man." The manifestation of his heavenly glory so oppressed him with fear, that he tells us in the 17th verse, "When I saw him, I fell at his feet as dead. And he laid his right hand upon me, saying unto me, Fear not; I am the first and the last." And he adds, "I am he that liveth, and was dead; and, behold, I am alive for evermore, Amen; and have the keys of hell and of death." In the second chapter, verse 8th, we read, "Unto the angel of the church in Smyrna write; These things saith the first and the last, which was dead, and is alive." Most plainly, then, is the crucified and risen Saviour the same person as "the first and the last." Again, in Revelation xxi. 6, after a description of the heavenly felicity, the Lord Jesus says, "It is done. I am Alpha and Omega, the beginning and the end;"

and a promise is subjoined which identifies the speaker at once; "I will give unto him that is athirst of the fountain of the water of life freely." For we read in John vii. 37, "In the last day, that great day of the feast, Jesus stood and cried, saying, If any man thirst, let him come unto me, and drink." And in Rev. xxii. 13, "I am Alpha and Omega, the beginning and the end, the first and the last," the context proves that the speaker is Jesus Christ.

We have thus referred to these six passages in the book of Revelation, because, taken together, they prove that our Lord assumes the attribute of eternity, and because we wish to consider three testimonies in the book of the prophet Isaiah, in juxtaposition with these remarkable passages.

In Isaiah xli. 4, Jehovah inquires, "Who hath wrought and done it, calling the generations from the beginning? I the Lord, the first, and with the last; I am he." In Isaiah xliv. 6, "Thus saith the Lord the King of Israel, and his redeemer the Lord of hosts; I am the first, and I am the last; and beside me there is no God." And in xlviii. 12, "Hearken unto me, O Jacob and Israel, my called; I am he; I am the first, I also am the last." No candid person can read these passages, and not be convinced that the speaker is Jehovah, the Lord of hosts; neither can it be denied that in the six passages in the book of Revelation, the Lord Jesus takes the title of "the first and the last." Therefore the Lord Jesus is co-equal and co-eternal with the Father, "Jehovah, the Lord of hosts."

Every proof of the Saviour's Deity is precious to the Christian. The foundation laid in Zion is a Divine foundation. The Saviour is a Divine Saviour. The atonement, the righteousness, and the sacrifice of the Lamb of God are Divine. Most consoling is it to reflect that there is an infinite efficacy and merit in the work of Christ, satisfying alike the requirements of perfect holiness and justice, and the trembling anxieties of a wounded and a spiritually enlightened conscience.

Let us now inquire what is set forth by the glorious title of the Lord Jesus, "I am Alpha and Omega."

The most cursory reader would gather from it an illustration of eternity. This is an attribute of God alone. All creatures have a beginning. God never had a beginning. The irrational creatures perish. Angels and men are immortal. The King of heaven is "immortal and invisible." Immortality, therefore, is not exclusively a prerogative of Deity, but eternity is. And Christ claims this to himself:

"I am Alpha and Omega." "In the beginning was the Word, and the Word was with God, and the Word was God. The same was in the beginning with God." "The Lord possessed me in the beginning of his way," Christ says in Proverbs viii. 22, "before his works of old. I was set up from everlasting, from the beginning, or ever the earth was. When there were no depths, I was brought forth; when there were no fountains abounding with water. Before the mountains were settled, before the hills, was I brought forth. While as yet he had not made the earth, nor the fields, nor the highest part of the dust of the world. When he prepared the heavens, I was there: when he set a compass upon the face of the depth: when he established the clouds above: when he strengthened the fountains of the deep: when he gave to the sea his decree, that the waters should not pass his commandment: when he appointed the foundations of the earth: then I was by him, as one brought up with him: and I was daily his delight, rejoicing always before him."

Let us examine our subject more in detail. Jesus Christ is the "Alpha and Omega" in *the department of Nature.* "All things were made by him; and without him was not anything made that was made." "By him were all things created, that are in heaven, and that are in earth, visible and invisible, whether they be thrones, or dominions, or principalities, or powers: all things were created by him, and for him: and he is before all things, and by him all things consist." In the beginning he laid the foundations of the earth, and the heavens were the work of his hands. He is the "Alpha" of creation. In him was "life," in him, as in a fountain; and from him, streams of life were distributed over the amplitude of his extensive dominions. He tenanted space with the countless luminaries of heaven, and impressed upon them, and upon our earth among them, that marvellous combination of opposing forces by which, with unerring precision, they have each retained their proper orbit. He framed and fashioned our globe, making it by successive dispensations meet for the residence of man; every plant, every tree, every animal, and man himself, were created by Jesus Christ in perfect maturity. The herb yielded its seed, the trees were laden with ripe fruit, the earth was clothed with luxuriant vegetation, and man was formed in the perfection of stature both of mind and body, in the image of God, "very good." And although, in the high purpose of God, sin has been permitted to enter, and to mar the handiwork of Christ, and to spread its withering curse around, and to introduce toil and sweat, thistles and thorns, diseases, decay, and death, amongst us; yet, even now, everywhere, we behold the footprints of Jesus Christ, the "Alpha and Omega" of creation. All that remains of beauty, and melody, and harmony, in the earth, is from him.

"By him all things consist." The "Alpha" of all, is also the "Omega." The Creator is also the sustainer, the upholder, and the perfecter. Every blade of grass, every ear of corn, all the fruits of autumn, every insect, born only for an hour's sunshine, every individual of the feathered and the finny tribes, and all the generations of men, have been formed and nourished by life and power from Christ. When he trode upon our earth, the sea, the grave, the clouds rendered due allegiance to him; and when he "shall come in his glory, and all the holy angels with him," he will, by a word, subdue his foes, and transfigure his people, and gather them from the four winds of heaven, and set up his monarchy of love, and peace, and righteousness, and reign King of kings and Lord of lords over a renovated universe. Of that blessed period, how sweetly does the poet sing!

> " See Salem built, the labour of a God ;
> Bright as a sun the sacred city shines.

All kingdoms and all princes of the earth
Flock to that light; the glory of all lands
Flows into her; unbounded is her joy;
Praise is in all her gates; upon her walls,
And in her streets, and in her spacious courts,
Is heard salvation. Eastern Java there
Kneels with the native of the furthest West,
And Ethiopia spreads abroad the hand,
And worships. Her report has travelled forth
Into all lands. From every clime they come
To see thy beauty, and to share thy joy,
Oh, Zion! an assembly such as earth
Saw never—such as Heaven stoops down to see."

Jesus Christ is the "Alpha and Omega" of the *arrangements of Providence.* Providence is that mighty scheme of Divine government by which all events, even the most minute, are ordered for the welfare of the church and for the glory of God. If all power is Christ's in heaven and earth, then all events of Providence are at his disposal. If he holds the keys of the invisible world, whether of bliss or of misery, and of death, as the portal through which the children of men pass one after another, then it follows that life is also under his sway. If heaven, hell, and death are governed by him, then life, with its momentous interests and responsibilities, its sorrows and its joys, must also be ordered by him.

The thought of Christ's sovereignty in providence is full of unspeakable comfort. By a wondrous course of discipline, Jacob was instructed in the ways of God. He learned by painful experience the bitterness of sin, and he was brought again and again to place his whole trust in the tender mercy and faithful promise of his God. In his dying benediction he left this testimony to the leadings of Providence. "God, before whom my fathers Abraham and Isaac did walk, the God which fed me all my life long unto this day, the Angel which redeemed me from all evil, bless the lads." Through what eventful vicissitudes was Joseph led; and with what tearful joy did he say to his penitent and astonished brethren, "Be not grieved, nor angry with yourselves, that ye sold me hither; for God did send me before you to save life." The charge of Moses to Israel was this: "Thou shalt remember all the way which the Lord thy God led thee these forty years in the wilderness, to humble thee, and to prove thee, to know what was in thine heart." And Joshua made this appeal: "Ye know in all your hearts, and in all your souls, that not one thing has failed of all the good things which the Lord your God spake concerning you." It is the privilege of the Christian, when he reviews the dealings of the Lord with his ancient people, to "thank God and take courage." The friend and guide of Jacob, and Joseph, and of the children of Israel, has pledged himself to be your friend and guide even unto death. Jesus Christ is "the first," he also is "with the last," even to the end of the world. The promises made to the saints of old, are assured to believers now. He who said to Joshua, "I will not fail thee, nor forsake thee," says to you, "I will never leave thee, nor forsake thee." "All the promises of God in him are yea, and in him amen, unto the glory of God by us."

Jesus Christ is your "Alpha and Omega" in providence. "He knoweth the end from the beginning." Your whole history is written out as on a map before him. The streams which you have to cross; the mountains over which you have to climb; the fertile valleys, rich with the grapes of Eshcol, where you shall enjoy sweet refreshment; and the long and dreary path in the wilderness into which sovereign wisdom shall allure you, ay, and where Jesus shall "speak comfortably" to you; and the dark river of Jordan, through whose swelling waters Divine love shall bear you, encircled within his everlasting embrace—all this way, from the beginning to the end, is ordered for you by the "Alpha and Omega, the beginning and the end." Art thou in sorrow, O Christian, and are thy days passed in grief and heaviness? Art thou laid upon a bed of languishing? Has God "stirred up thy nest?" Has he broken up thy home, torn down the walls of thy habitation, and permitted the searching winds of adversity to sigh through its ruins? Art thou straitened, oppressed, and desolate? Is it that no one knows thee? and when thou dost look forward, are all thine earthly prospects shrouded in the thickest gloom? Fear not: death is the womb of life. If thou art a child of the living God, all thy present discipline is "big with mercy." All the attributes of God are exercised in thy behalf and for thy welfare. He who has loved thee from everlasting, shall love thee to everlasting. The end shall crown the way, thy home shall abundantly compensate the preparatory discipline. The "Alpha" of thy faith and hope, will be the "Omega" of thy joy.

Jesus Christ is the "Alpha and Omega" in the system of grace.

"Look at the *revelation of Divine grace in the Scriptures.* Christ is the "Alpha and Omega" of the Bible. Of him the first verse in Genesis, and the last verse in Revelation, bear witness. The Bible is the centre of theology. The gospel is the centre of the Bible. Jesus Christ is the centre of the gospel: in him the types of the Mosaic ritual are fulfilled: to him the sacrifices of the law referred: of him the prophets testified, and psalmists chanted sweet songs of praise. Apostles and evangelists wrote memoirs of his humiliation, and in their preaching and letters they knew nothing save "Jesus Christ and him crucified," Jesus Christ and him glorified.

Look at the *origin*, *development*, and *completion of the system of grace* towards our world. Of this system Christ is the "Alpha." The vessels of mercy were chosen in Christ before the foundation of the world, and "given to him" by the Father as "a people for his praise." At the fall, the promise of a Redeemer was made; and four thousand years after, the promise was fulfilled, and the hopes of ten thousand times ten thousand saints were realized. "When the fulness of the time was come, God sent forth his Son, made of a woman, made under the law." "The Word was made flesh, and dwelt among us." Christ magnified the law, and made it honourable by a sinless obedience and by a voluntary submission to its penalty. "He bare our sins in his own body on the tree." He rose from the dead for our justification. He is at the right hand of God, where he "maketh intercession for us." From his mediatorial throne, he pours out his blessings upon men. Though "exalted far above all principality and power," he ever proves himself the sympathizing friend of his people. He has watched over his church from age to age, and has never withdrawn his presence from her. In the darkest periods he has not left himself without witness. But in these latter times, the testimony for Jesus is greatly multiplied. The missionaries of the cross traverse the remotest regions of the earth, and carry the message of Divine love to nations whose very existence was not known to our forefathers. God is now visiting the Gentiles, and he is gathering out to himself from the land of Sinim, and from the gold fields of Australia; from the arid plains of Hindostan, and the spicy groves of Ceylon; from the vast continent of Africa, and the islands of the Pacific; from the extensive plains of America; from ice-bound Labrador; and last, but not least, from the neglected masses of our own baptized heathen at home, stars of righteousness and jewels of glory. And that Saviour, whose cross has been the central point of attraction to his people, in all climes and through all periods, is coming, as the grand "Omega" of Christianity; not in weakness, but in power; not in humiliation, but in majesty; not as "the Man of sorrows," but as the King of glory.

Look at the *work of grace in the heart and life of the believer*. Christ is the "Alpha," the "Author of our faith." The first movement of the heart towards God, is *of* God. By the still small voice of the Spirit, Christ speaks *in* man. Providence, sermons, and religious books speak *to* man. The Spirit of Christ speaks in the heart gently, but with power. A soft voice in the house is heard more distinctly than a loud cry in the street. This is general, that is special; this is to the multitude, that to the individual. Various are the means employed, but the great agent is the same. Under divers circumstances are men called: Samuel, in the hour of still repose; Josiah, amid the urgent claims of public life; Matthew, at the receipt of custom; Peter, at his fishing; Saul, on his way to Damascus; Lydia, the purple-seller of Thyatira, at the meeting for prayer by the river side, and the thief on the cross, were all called by the one Spirit. The first step is from God. "No man cometh to me, except the Father which hath sent me draw him." "I have loved thee with an everlasting love; therefore with loving-kindness have I drawn thee." "We love him, because he first loved us." "Thy people shall be willing in the day of thy power." If we "look unto the rock whence we were hewn, and to the hole of the pit whence we were digged," we shall acknowledge that it was so in our own experience. If we be asked, How is the voice of the Spirit of Jesus to be distinguished from the voice of conscience? we may answer, the voice of conscience may be subdued and silenced. The voice of the Spirit speaks again and again, more and more powerfully, until the strong man armed is humbled effectually before the cross. Conscience may deter from sin, excite to the performance of duty, and, when thoroughly aroused, may goad a man to despair. Thus it was with Saul and Judas. But the Holy Spirit convinces of sin, in order that he may convince of righteousness. He wounds that he may heal. He leads the sinner sweetly and yet mightily from the love of the world and the crushing power of sin, to the cross, to holiness, and to heaven.

Christ, then, is the "Alpha" of our conversion. "By grace are ye saved through faith; and that not of yourselves: it is the gift of God." As the first step is from Christ, so every succeeding step in our heavenly journey is from him. "As ye have therefore received Christ Jesus the Lord, so walk ye in him: rooted and built up in him." Without Christ we can do nothing. In repentance, in faith, in obedience, in patient endurance, we are powerless without him. This is a daily lesson. What are we in secret prayer, in the path of duty, in the conflict with corruption, in our walk before God? What are we without Jesus Christ but whited sepulchres, pieces of clay, hard and cold and stupid as the stones of the valley?

The most blessed life on this side heaven, is that of continual dependence upon Christ. Experience alone can enable us to realize how sweet and how endearing it is, in every duty, emergency, and sorrow, to go to Jesus Christ, as a child to a tender parent, and in faith and submission to spread our case before him. By his word, he speaks to our hearts; by his appointed ordinances, he bestows upon us his grace; by his beautiful works in nature, and by the strange yet faithful dealings of his providence, he teaches us about himself. And we may, we do hold communion with him, not only at stated seasons, but in sudden ejaculations, such as "Lord, save me;" "Lord, help me;" "O Lord, I beseech thee, deliver my soul;" "O my God, remember me for good." Throughout, Christ is our "all and in all;" "wisdom and righteousness, sanctification and redemption." "The path of the just is as the shining light, that shineth more and more unto the perfect day." "The righteous shall hold on his way." And when the work of grace is completed, and the sands of life are run out, then will Christ the "Author" be the "Finisher of our faith." In the last struggle, he will be with us, and his rod and his staff shall comfort us. He has given us grace to live; he will give us grace to die. He will smooth our pillow, and bid the enemy keep far from us. He will bear up our fainting spirit, and carry us in peace, if not in triumph and ecstasy, to our eternal home, where we shall for ever sing, "Unto him that loved us, and washed us from our sins in his own blood, and hath made us kings and priests unto God and his Father, to him be glory and dominion for ever and ever. Amen."

JESUS.

"I am Jesus."—ACTS ix. 5.

ON two occasions the Saviour claimed this blessed name to himself; in the garden, at his apprehension, when his enemies "went backward, and fell to the ground;" and in heaven, when from his throne he beheld the danger of his disciples in Damascus; and the lion, Saul of Tarsus, "breathing out threatenings and slaughter," was transformed into the lamb, and was struck to the earth by the words, "Saul, Saul, why persecutest thou me? And he said, Who art thou, Lord? And the Lord said, I am Jesus, whom thou persecutest: it is hard for thee to kick against the pricks."

This name was given to the Saviour by the angel before he was conceived in the womb. Its meaning was added by the inspired evangelist, "for he shall save his people from their sins. Now all this was done, that it might be fulfilled which was spoken of the Lord by the prophet, saying, Behold, a virgin shall be with child, and shall bring forth a son, and they shall call his name Emmanuel, which being interpreted is, God with us." We infer then that "Jesus" means *God the Saviour* — an inference which is confirmed by the investigation of the name itself. "Jesus" is the Greek form of the name "Joshua." In fact, it is put for Joshua in Heb. iv. 8: "For if Jesus had given them rest, then would he not afterward have spoken of another day." The full meaning of Joshua is God the Saviour, which has been ably shown by Bishop Pearson. Joshua was a remarkable type of Christ. Moses could only bring the Israelites to the river Jordan; Joshua must lead them into the promised land. "The law was our schoolmaster to bring us to Christ." "The law was given by Moses, but grace and truth came by Jesus Christ." Joshua led the Israelites on dry ground, through the river Jordan, at a season when it always overflowed its banks. The Lord Jesus brings his people through the "swellings of Jordan," and enables them to triumph over death and hell. Under Joshua, the people of the Lord conquered the Canaanites, and were settled in their several inheritances, each tribe in its predestinated portion. Through Jesus, we are more than conquerors over our spiritual enemies, and we shall in due course enter into the rest of heaven, the kingdom prepared for believers before the foundation of the world. But every type falls far short of the reality, even as the earthly must ever be far inferior to the heavenly. The salvation wrought by Joshua was but temporal; that wrought by Jesus Christ is eternal. One nation only was benefited by Joshua; in Jesus Christ, all the families of the earth are blessed. In a good old age, Joshua died and was gathered to his fathers; "Christ being raised from the dead dieth no more: death hath no more dominion over him." He is "alive for evermore."

Let us now inquire, From what has Jesus saved us? In what manner? And on what grounds may we hope to obtain an interest in his salvation? Jesus "saves his people from their sins,"—from the guilt of sin, from the power of sin, and from the condemnation of sin. The guilt of sin exposes us to the wrath of God; the power of sin enslaves us under the tyranny of Satan; the condemnation of sin results in the miseries of hell. Jesus Christ saves us from the wrath of God, from the yoke of Satan, and from the agonies of damnation.

"Sin is the transgression of the law." It has "brought death into the world, and all our woe."

It drove Satan and his legions from heaven, and our first parents from Eden; it destroyed the old world; it overthrew the cities of the plain; it slew the Canaanitish nations; it reduced the house of Israel to a banishment, that shall only terminate at the Lord's second coming; it imprisoned the house of Judah in Babylon for seventy years; and for eighteen centuries the wrath of God has scattered the Jews over the earth, "a hissing, a proverb, and a reproach to all nations." Sin has subverted the haughtiest empires: Nineveh, Babylon, Persepolis, and Rome have crumbled under its sway. It drowned Pharaoh in the Red Sea; drove Nebuchadnezzar to eat grass with the beasts of the field; it devoured Herod with worms. It has made this earth of ours, so beautiful even under the curse, like a vast hospital, full of mourning, lamentation, and woe. In a word, it has peopled earth with the children of sorrow, and hell with the children of despair. But if we would contemplate sin in its most awful aspect, we must draw near to Calvary. Whom do we behold stretched upon the accursed tree? What is the title over the cross?—"Jesus of Nazareth, the king of the Jews." Yes, be astonished, O heavens; and hear, O earth; "God so loved the world, that he gave his only begotten Son." He who spared Abraham's son, did not spare his own Son. When we were enemies, Christ died for us, "the Just for the unjust, that he might bring us to God." Behold the crucified One. Think upon the sufferings of his body, and the sorrows that drank up his spirit. Think upon his eternal dignity, and his spotless innocence; and behold in the cross the deepest proof of the guilt and malignity of sin, the grandest illustration of Divine holiness, and the mightiest achievement of Divine love.

Sin is bondage. Evil habits are the chains with which Satan binds his willing captives. Ahab "sold himself to work wickedness." Sinners make their own chains, and work out their own ruin. "Woe unto them that draw iniquity with cords of vanity, and sin as it were with a cart-rope." There is a formidable growth in the power of sin. At first it was as fine as a hempen string; habit twisted it into a cord of vanity; and time strengthens the cord into a rope of iniquity. How awful are the apostle's words, "Lust, when it hath conceived, bringeth forth sin; and sin, when it is finished, bringeth forth death!" and how solemn is the prophet's question, "Can the Ethiopian change his skin, or the leopard his spots? Then may ye also do good, that are accustomed to do evil!" Sin paralyses man's soul. "I well remember," said a clergyman in London, "one wintry night, when the storm was raging and the wind was howling, being called up to attend one who was in the agonies of death, and who had long been living an avowed life of sin. But he became anxious at last to know if it were possible for him to find a place of safety; and never shall I forget the answer which that poor dying man made to me when I directed him to pray. 'Pray! sir,' he said; '*I cannot pray.* I have lived in sin too long to pray; I cannot—I know not how; and if this be all, I must perish.'" Such is the effect of long-continued, habitual sin.

Sin brings its own condemnation. The wages of sin is death—temporal, spiritual, and eternal death. At the great day, the sinner will be self-condemned as well as law-condemned. The man who had not accepted and put on the proffered wedding garment "was speechless." Sinners now are so careless that they have not a word to say *to* God; then they will be so conscience-stricken that they shall not have a word to say *before* God. When the Judge shall pass the sentence, "Depart from me, ye cursed, into everlasting fire, prepared for the devil and his angels," their burning tongues will be constrained to acknowledge, "Just and true are thy ways," O

Lord God of hosts. Fools make a mock of sin here, but sin will make a mock of them hereafter. Shame and everlasting contempt, weeping, wailing, and gnashing of teeth, fire and brimstone, storm and tempest, shall be their portion, for "the wicked shall be turned into hell, and all the nations that forget God."

From the condemnation, power, and guilt of sin, Jesus Christ saves those who believe in him. Our next inquiry is into the *manner* in which this has been brought about.

By faith in his blood and righteousness, we obtain a *title* to salvation. God gave man a law. That law was a transcript of his Divine mind; it was holy, just, and good. God required a perfect obedience—an obedience which would insure our happiness and his glory. In default of this obedience, there was a penalty. That penalty was death. "The soul that sinneth, it shall die." Man, by transgression, fell, and lost his high estate. Corrupt in heart, alienated in mind, and disobedient in practice, how could he stand before a holy God? How escape the awful penalty? How fulfil the requisite obedience? Justice—stern, unbending justice—demands the execution of the penalty. Mercy—sweet and gentle mercy—weeps, and pleads that sinners should be forgiven and lifted up to glory. But how are these contending parties to be reconciled? Shall the high and lofty One dishonour his law, tarnish his justice, and falsify his word? Impossible. Are sinners, then, to be swept, generation after generation, into the abyss of despair? Where, then, is mercy? Mercy weeps again, because when she looks upon the families of men, she can find no advocate, no intercessor. This was the difficulty. The wisdom, love, and power of the eternal Trinity devised the solution of the mighty problem. Jesus undertook to be our surety and substitute. He agreed in covenant with the Father and the Holy Spirit to take, in the "fulness of time," the human nature into union with the Divine nature, and to fulfil the double requirement of the law—its obedience and its penalty. All this he graciously accomplished. By his Holy Spirit, he took our nature, and was "born of a pure virgin." For thirty-three years he tabernacled with men. He was "holy, harmless, undefiled, separate from sinners." He magnified the law and made it honourable, and brought in an everlasting righteousness. On the cross, he suffered as the surety for man. "All we like sheep have gone astray; we have turned every one to his own way: and the

Lord hath laid on him the iniquity of us all." "God was in Christ, reconciling the world unto himself, not imputing their trespasses unto them. For he hath made him to be sin for us, who knew no sin, that we might be made the righteousness of God in him." Hence, in his prayer in the garden, he could say, "Father, I have glorified thee on the earth, I have finished the work that thou gavest me to do;" and on the cross, he could exclaim in triumph, "It is finished." Jesus has bought our *title* to salvation. He has put the highest honour upon all the attributes of God; he has satisfied all the necessities of guilty, ruined sinners. "Thanks be unto God for his unspeakable gift."

But Christ has done more than this for us. Through faith in his atonement, we obtain our title to heaven. But what would this avail, if we had been left to make ourselves holy and fit for heaven? We must have *meetness* for, as well as the title to heaven. Suppose you had a son, and you forbade him to enter a place of contagion, on pain of losing all you could leave him. He goes, and is seized with the infection. He thus is not only guilty, by transgressing your command, but he is also diseased. And do you not perceive that your *forgiving* him does not *heal* him? He wants not only the father's pardon, but the physician's aid; and in vain is he freed from the forfeiture of his estate, if he be left under the power of his disorder. Christ is our Physician. By his Spirit he subdues our sins, and quickens us to holy obedience; he imparts to us a new principle of life; we are "made new creatures in Christ Jesus;" he "has ascended on high; he has led captivity captive; he has received gifts for men, yea, for the rebellious also, that the Lord God might dwell among them." The Holy Spirit is now given, because Jesus is now glorified. To this the apostle refers when he says, "If, when we were enemies, we were reconciled to God by the death of his Son: much more, being reconciled, we shall be saved by his life." Behold then the riches of Divine grace. See how the wisdom of God originated the wondrous plan, and how the power of God perfected it. See how the Deity of Jesus gives an infinite merit to his obedience and his sacrifice. See how the humanity of Jesus gives him the capacity to do and to suffer the will of God. See how, on Calvary, "Mercy and truth met together; righteousness and peace kissed each other." See how Christ sanctifies those whom he saves; in short, how the guilt of sin is pardoned, how the power of sin is broken; and how "there is no condemnation to them which are in Christ Jesus, who walk not after the flesh, but after the Spirit."

On what grounds may we hope to obtain an interest in the salvation of Jesus Christ? His promise, his power, and his love.

His *promise* binds him to confer it upon us, if we ask him. Jesus has condescended to pledge himself to penitent souls, by "exceeding great and precious promises." "Come unto me, all ye that labour and are heavy laden, and I will give you rest." "He that believeth in the Son hath everlasting life." "Him that cometh to me I will in no wise cast out." "Let the wicked forsake his way, and the unrighteous man his thoughts: and let him return unto the Lord, and he will have mercy upon him; and to our God, for he will abundantly pardon." Invitations and promises like these might be quoted from every part of the Bible. By these Christ has been pleased to bind himself. He is the "Amen, the faithful and true witness." "Heaven and earth may pass away, but one jot or one tittle shall in no wise pass from the law, till all be fulfilled." Has his word ever been broken? Let fulfilled prophecy answer. Let saints in heaven answer. Let believers on earth bear witness. Go and ask any servant of the living God. What will be the reply? "I have been unfaithful to my Lord ten thousand times, but Christ has never been unfaithful to me; he has never disappointed me; he has ever exceeded my expectations. I can set to my seal that God is *true*." How pleasant is the testimony of a well-used Bible! Here you see a broad mark to draw attention; there a date written, to recall some incident in experience; perhaps you see a mark on the margin of some text, and it means that that text contains a precious promise. Such texts have been like a rock for the trembling feet; such words of life have been tried and proved, and have never failed to afford direction, comfort, and hope. Art thou an inquirer after the Saviour? Art thou afraid to draw near to him? Fear not, "be of good cheer; rise, he calleth thee." Take his own invitation and his promise. Plead them in earnest prayer. Act like the Christian negro, who said, "I fall flat on the promise, and I pray straight up." Let this be your plea: Lord, such is thy promise to the poor, the weak, the guilty, the penitent. "Do as thou hast said." "Thou saidst, I will surely do thee good." Fulfil thine own promise, in thine own time.

His *power* enables him to grant that which he has promised. Jesus is able to "save his people from their sins." Man's promise may fail, through change of circumstances and want of ability. Christ is an unchangeable Saviour. He has almighty power. Is not this consolatory to the inquirer? Have your sins been as numerous as the sands upon the sea-shore? "The blood of Jesus Christ cleanseth from all sin." Are your evil habits like chains of adamant about your soul? Christ is able to subdue sin and to trample down Satan for you and in you. "Look unto me, and be ye saved, all the ends of the earth; for I am God, and there is none else."

The *love* of Christ inclines him to save sinners. There is no want of power with him; neither is he unwilling. For he is love. "Have I any pleasure at all that the wicked should die? saith the Lord God." What brought him on his errand of mercy to our earth? Love to the lost. What made him willing to resign for a season the adoration of heaven, that he might sojourn with man? Love to the lost. What made him willing to endure privation, poverty, the ignorance of the people, the contempt of the Pharisees, and the unbelief of his own disciples? Love to the lost. What inclined him to make an atonement, and to bear the sins of men upon the cross? Love to the lost. What has induced him to carry on the gracious work in heaven, and to plead for sinners with his Father? Love to the lost. Do you not know some one person (perhaps you may know many such) who prayed to Jesus, and who has found a sweet welcome and a free pardon? What inclined Him to extend mercy to that individual? Love to the lost. What he has done for others, he will do for you. He has never cast out a returning wanderer: he will not cast you out. Doubt not then his willingness to save. The leper "worshipped him, saying, Lord, if thou wilt, thou canst make me clean; and Jesus put forth his hand, and touched him, saying, I will; be thou clean. And immediately his leprosy was cleansed." If Christ had been unwilling to save sinners, he would not have died for them. If he had been unwilling to save you, he would have been unwilling to save others like you. But he is not unwilling. The very fact of your preservation to the present hour is a proof of his patience and forbearance towards you. And patient long-suffering implies love to the lost and a willingness to save; you have therefore every ground of encouragement to draw you to Jesus Christ. "The Spirit and the bride say, Come. And let him that heareth say, Come. And let him that is athirst come. And whosoever will, let him take the water of life freely." His faithfulness, his power, and his love bid you welcome: "Come, for all things are now ready."

The name of Jesus is full of consolation to the Christian, because it reminds him of the state of guilt and misery in which grace found him; of the amazing cost at which salvation was purchased; and of the relief, pardon, and satisfaction which he experienced when he first "fled for refuge to lay hold upon the hope set before us" in the gospel. The name of Jesus is sweet, as memory retraces the story of life—not of life according to the flesh, but of life according to the spirit. We acknowledge with shame, and yet with thankfulness, that we have *lived*, only since we have loved Jesus. "To me to live is Christ." And the story of life tells, how the name of Jesus has been an inexhaustible spring of peace and joy; how it has driven back many temptations, dried many tears, and healed many sorrows; how in some spiritual conflict and perplexity, the Holy Ghost has whispered the name of Jesus in the heart, and it has been like the rising of the sun, which has dispersed the clouds of sin and unbelief; how when the cross had to be taken up in some peculiar call of duty, and nature, always self-indulgent, recoiled, how the name of Jesus has banished every fear and nerved us for the task; and how when in faith and obedience we went straight to the work, anticipating only roughness and difficulty, we found such a hallowed sweetness, that, as it was once said by an eminent minister, "The very cross that we took up for Jesus, was lined with velvet."

There have been seasons of communion with our fellow Christians, when the name of Jesus has been "as ointment poured forth." Our hearts have burned within us whilst he, alas! too often an unknown friend in the midst of us, has opened to our minds the promises of the word respecting himself. "Our hearts have mingled into bliss," as we have spoken of him whom we love, and as we have testified to each other of his grace to our souls.

In his house, and at his table, how sweet have we found his name! Often have we said, "This is none other than the house of God, and this is the gate of heaven." "He brought me to the banqueting house, and his banner over me was love."

Never, perhaps, do we realize the sweetness of the name of Jesus more than when we bend over the dying bed of a true Christian. In such a chamber God holds his court, and we feel a solemn reverence spread over our spirit, and that we are on holy ground. Disease has been taking down the earthly tabernacle, pin by pin, and there is scarcely a stake to be removed. But while the outward man perishes, the inward man has been renewed from day to day. The pale countenance is lighted up with heavenly peace, and the eye glistens with consolation all divine. Do we ask, "Are you happy?" "Yes," is the prompt reply, "happy in Jesus; Jesus is mine, and I am his." "Have you any fear of death?" "No, for Jesus is with me; I will fear no evil; his rod and his staff comfort me." "Do you depend upon anything in yourself, any sacrifice you have made for Christ, or any services which you have rendered to his cause?" "No, no; my best is stained and dyed with sin, my all is nothing worth; my whole trust is in the precious blood and perfect righteousness of Jesus; he is my all and in all." Have we not witnessed such a scene again and again? Has not the testimony to the grace of Jesus been most solemnizing and elevating? Have we not prayed as we lingered in the chamber, where angels hovered around, waiting for the word of command to bear the emancipated spirit to the rest above, "Let me die the death of the righteous, and let my last end be like his?" If the name of Jesus has been sweet in life, will it not be unspeakably sweet in the strife of death? How blessed then to have a Saviour to rejoice in, and not a Saviour to seek! And if Jesus' name will be so sweet in the last struggle, what will be our emotions of wonder, love, and praise, if we are found in him at the great day, amid the throes of a universe travailing with fire for the bringing forth the new heavens and new earth! What will be our ascription of praise when we find our poor unworthy names written in the Lamb's book of life, and mentioned with gracious distinction by the Judge of quick and dead!

Reader, is Christ precious to you? Do you trust in him and love him? If not, why not?

"MESSIAS."

"The woman saith unto him, I know that Messias cometh, which is called Christ: when he is come, he will tell us all things. Jesus saith unto her, I that speak unto thee am he." —JOHN iv. 25, 26.

MESSIAH and Christ both signify "the Anointed One." Messiah is the Hebrew, Messias the Syriac, and Christ is the Greek form of the same word. The woman of Samaria said, "I know that Messias cometh." Andrew saith to his brother Simon, "We have found the Messias." The woman and Andrew both spoke in the Syriac or Syro-Chaldaic language. John wrote in Greek, the universal language of that day, as English or French is in our day, and therefore he explained Messias by adding, "which is called Christ," and by commonly writing Christ instead of Messias in his gospel. Messias, then, is the same with Christ. Anointing with oil, was the ancient form of consecration to the service of God. At Bethel, "Jacob poured oil upon the top of the stone which he set up for a pillar," and he said, "This stone, which I have set for a pillar, shall be God's house." Moses anointed the tabernacle, and all the vessels with oil, and thus set them apart for the service of Almighty God. Prophets, priests, and kings were anointed at their installation into their sacred office. The Lord Jesus was anointed, not with material oil, but with the Holy Ghost; not by the hand of man, but by God himself, as the head of his true church, the Prophet, Priest, and King of his people. In his first sermon at Nazareth, he announced this holy unction, "The Spirit of the Lord is upon me, because he hath anointed me to preach the gospel to the poor; he hath sent me to heal the broken-hearted, to preach deliverance to the captives, and recovering of sight to the blind, to set at liberty them that are bruised, to preach the acceptable year of the Lord. And he closed the book, and he gave it again to the minister, and sat down. And the eyes of all them that were in the synagogue were fastened on him. And he began to say unto them, This day is this Scripture fulfilled in your ears." And to the woman of Samaria he said, "I that speak unto thee am" the true Messias.

Let us glance at some of the proofs of the Messiahship of Jesus of Nazareth; and then meditate upon the blessings which accrue to his church from his threefold office of Prophet, Priest, and King. There was, at the time when Jesus appeared, a very general expectation among the Jews of the Messiah. This expectation had spread among other nations. Philip said to Nathanael, "We have found him, of whom Moses in the law, and the prophets, did write, Jesus of Nazareth, the son of Joseph." The woman of Samaria expresses the general feeling, "We know that Messias cometh." The people said, "When Christ cometh, no man knoweth whence he is;" and some of his disciples said, "When Christ cometh, will he do more miracles than those which this man hath done?" When John the Baptist entered upon his ministry, and preached with such astonishing power and success, Luke tells us, that "all men mused in their hearts of John, whether he were the Christ or not." Many more proofs might be mentioned of the expectation of the Messiah which pervaded the Jewish mind. The visit of the Magi shows how far eastward this opinion had spread, and the testimony of classical writers proves that the civilized nations of the West entertained the same idea. The promises of the seed to the early patriarchs; the predictions of

Moses; and the stream of prophecy which flowed in one continuous and unbroken channel for six hundred years from Samuel to Malachi, more or less referring all along to the coming of Christ, would naturally make a strong impression upon the Jewish people. The settlement of many Jews, after the Babylonish captivity, in the regions of Asia, in Egypt, and in the bordering countries, would spread the knowledge of the true God, and of that prominent article of their creed, the expectation of a Messiah, through the heathen world. The peculiarity of their manners, the purity and comparative spirituality of their worship, the high antiquity of their sacred books, and the marvellous dealings of Jehovah with their nation in past ages, would bespeak, nay, command the attention of the heathen to their doctrines and their hopes. In addition to this, prophecy had fixed a definite point of time for the coming of the Messiah. The celebrated prediction of the seventy weeks or four hundred and ninety prophetic years tied down their expectation to the very period when Jesus of Nazareth did appear and minister among them.

The *miracles* of Christ were the great proof of his Divine mission to which he always referred. "The works which I do in my Father's name, they bear witness of me." These miracles were performed in public; thousands witnessed them, and could not be mistaken in, or deceived by them; they were wrought in different places, and were marked by a singular variety; they were many in number. The Jews relate seventy-four miracles by Moses, and seventy-six by the prophets; but John tells us that if all the things were written that Jesus did, "even the world itself could not contain the books that should be written." The bitterest enemies of the Lord never denied the performance of these miracles; but they ascribed them to Satanic agency—a horrible blasphemy, which the Saviour himself refuted in an unanswerable manner.

The *prophecies* in the Old Testament have been minutely fulfilled in Jesus of Nazareth, and in no one else. The Jews who crucified him, and who persecuted his followers from city to city, have been the librarians of these sacred oracles. Most jealously have they watched over the sacred deposit. No apprehension, therefore, need be felt that the evangelists corrupted the Old Testament to adapt its prophecies to Jesus of Nazareth. Neither could or would an impostor have fulfilled these predictions in himself. A man cannot arrange the place of his birth, nor the particular mother, nor family of which he is to be born. No mere man could perform the variety of miracles that Jesus wrought. Neither would an impostor have been diligent to fulfil predictions which involved his own persecution, contempt, betrayal, crucifixion (with its minute details), and consequent death. If it be thought possible that an impostor would submit to all this in order to make for himself a name in the world, and to establish his own system, we may answer that no impostor would have made such sacrifices with such slender hopes and prospects. At his crucifixion, the disciples of Jesus were but a few illiterate individuals who had all forsaken him; and the whole Jewish nation was mad with disappointed rage against him. Under such circumstances, would Jesus have yielded himself to crucifixion if he had been an ordinary man or an impostor?

But the *character* of our Lord alone would be sufficient to refute such a calumny. Was not his whole demeanour a specimen of Divine goodness and purity walking up and down in the midst of us? Could he not fearlessly challenge his adversaries, "Which of you convinceth me of sin?" Was not his transparent holiness and integrity one secret of the power with which he taught? Some have thought that if Virtue herself should ever walk upon this earth, all mankind would immediately kneel down and worship her. Alas for poor human nature! Plato had a deeper insight into the weakness and malice of man, for, speaking of the treatment which the good man would receive, he said that "he would be tortured, spit upon, have his two eyes put out, and finally, he would be crucified." What a remarkable testimony is this from a heathen writer who lived more than three centuries before the birth of Christ!

We have not space to enter more at length into the evidences for the Messiahship of Jesus. We have only alluded in the briefest manner to one or two proofs; and those who would pursue a most inviting field of profitable investigation are referred to the works of Paley, Sumner, Davison, Keith, and a host of writers who have regarded it as their highest honour to dedicate their talents and attainments to their Saviour's cause, and to the vindication of his holy religion.

We would close what we have said by turning to one or two passages of Scripture. In Genesis xlix. 10, we read: "The sceptre shall not depart from Judah, nor a lawgiver from between his feet, until Shiloh come; and unto him shall the gathering of the people be." If Jesus be not the true Messiah, the true Shiloh, the "Sent" of God, no one else can be: for the Jews have lost their sceptre, and their lawgiver, their civil and ecclesiastical polity for more than eighteen hundred years. And that "the people," the heathen nations, have been gathered to Jesus, the propagation of Christianity is an abundant witness.

In Malachi iii. 1: "Behold, I will send my messenger, and he shall prepare the way before me: and the Lord, whom ye seek, shall suddenly come to his temple, even the messenger of the covenant, whom ye delight in: behold, he shall come, saith the Lord of hosts." And in Haggai ii. 7: "I will shake all nations, and the desire of all nations shall come: and I will fill this house with glory, saith the Lord of hosts." The appearance of Messiah was thus fastened to the second temple. "I will fill *this* house with glory." If Jesus were not the true Messiah, no one else can be, for the temple was laid in ruins forty years after his ascension, and since that time the Jews have been exiles and wanderers, the witnesses to the truth of Jehovah in all the world.

In Jeremiah xxiii. 5: "Behold, the days come, saith the Lord, that I will raise unto David a righteous Branch." From this, and a multitude of similar texts, we gather that the Messiah was to be the son of David. At the time when our Lord was born, the genealogies of the Jews were preserved with scrupulous exactness, and we have a double list of the ancestors of Jesus in the Gospels, tracing up his lineage to David on his mother's side, and on his reputed father's side. But we think if any one should now appear among the Jews, claiming to be their Messiah, it would be difficult and well-nigh impossible for him to prove his genealogy to David. From the present state of the Jews, therefore, and from the rapid and unexampled growth of Christianity, we may, independently of the arguments from miracles, prophecy, or our Lord's character, obtain conclusive proofs that Jesus is the Christ, the Anointed Prophet, Priest, and King of his true church. We think that no serious reader will regret the attention which he has given to these evidences, because it is the solemn duty of every Christian to be able "to give a reason of the hope that is in him with meekness and fear," and with all charity "to refute gainsayers;" and further, there are seasons when we are assaulted with the poisoned shafts of infidelity, and when it is expedient to have the mind well stored with facts, and scriptural arguments, with which to drive back the enemy of souls.

Great and manifold are the blessings which flow to the church from the threefold office of her Divine Head.

Jesus Christ is the true *Prophet.* The ancient seers were commissioned directly by God to instruct, encourage, and warn his chosen people; and to predict future events. The Lord Jesus was a "teacher sent from God." And he foretold his own death and resurrection; the destruction of Jerusalem; and, in the book of Revelation, the history of his church to the end of time. In him were the celebrated words of Moses accomplished, "The Lord thy God will raise up unto thee a prophet from the midst of thee, of thy brethren, like unto me; unto him ye shall hearken." Let us consider the Lord Jesus as the great Teacher. How weighty were his lessons! He "brought life and immortality to light." The importance of faith; the straitness of the gate, and the narrowness of the way; the necessity of self-denial; the duties of prayer, watchfulness, humility, and forgiveness, were his topics. How simple and appropriate were his illustrations! The corn fields, the lilies, the processes of sowing and fishing supplied him with materials. How kind was his manner! What tenderness to the young, and what sympathy for the afflicted did he evince! What encouragement to the timid, and what commendation to the meek and diligent did he minister! How faithful were his warnings! What wisdom, majesty, and grace shone in his discourses! Well might the officers remark, "Never man spake like this man." His example was as pure and perfect as his teaching was grave and holy. He taught by life as well as by lip. He rose early for secret prayer. It was his meat and drink to do his Father's will. Never did he speak an idle word. Everywhere the Word and Wisdom of God was "holy, harmless, undefiled, separate from sinners." He went into society, and he sanctified it. He attended at a wedding ceremonial, and there manifested his glory. He withdrew from the multitude when they desired to clothe him with the pomp and insignia of earthly royalty. His delight was with the children of suffering and sorrow.

What is the testimony of believers to his teaching? Are they not witnesses to his grace, patience, and faithfulness? Cannot they say, "Who teacheth like him?" "I am the Lord thy God which teacheth thee to profit, which leadeth thee by the way thou shouldest go." When he spoke by his Spirit in our hearts, was it not with power? When he opened our eyes, did we not perceive wondrous things in his word? When he took us in hand, did we not learn more in five minutes than in all our past life from human teachers? Has he not taught us many lessons by his rod? Cannot we testify that his teaching is suitable, and holy, and full of sweetest joy? And his instructions in the sanctuary, and at his table, have they not distilled like dew into our souls, and made us fruitful in every good word and work? Can the reader attest all this in his own experience? If so, let him adore the riches of sovereign grace. If not, how earnestly would we exhort him, Oh taste and see how gracious the Lord is! "The meek will he guide in judgment; and the meek will he teach his way."

Jesus Christ is our "merciful and faithful *High Priest.*" Under the law, the priests were washed in water, and anointed with oil, at their entrance into their holy function. The Lord Jesus was consecrated by his baptism in Jordan, and by the anointing of the Holy Ghost for his office, as Priest of his church. In a general way, we may observe that the duties of the Levitical priests were three: sacrifice, intercession, benediction. Christ was at once our priest, altar, and victim. He offered up himself. He hath taken away sin by the sacrifice of himself. His Divinity was the altar, his humanity was the victim, he himself, both God and man, was the sacrificing priest. The legal sacrifices were frequently repeated. Christ offered himself *once.* Those sacrifices consisted of bulls and calves which could never take away sin. Christ "bare our sins in his own body on the tree." Those sacrifices availed only to remove ceremonial pollution; Christ's sacrifice appeases the troubled conscience, and reconciles the penitent to his offended Father, and cleanseth from all sin. "By him all that believe are justified from all things, from which they could not be justified by the law of Moses."

Having sprinkled the blood upon and before the mercy-seat seven times, the high priest presented the incense in the golden censer, and the fragrant cloud ascended before the Lord in the holy of holies. Our High Priest having taken his mediatorial throne in the highest heavens, pleads in behalf of his people, "his agony and bloody sweat, his cross and passion," and intercedes for them with "his Father and their Father, with his God and their God." When he came forth to bless the waiting congregation, the high priest clothed himself with his "garments of beauty." At his return to our earth "to be glorified in his saints, and to be admired in all them that believe," the Lord Jesus shall be clothed with celestial splendour; he shall wear a diadem of surpassing glory: "Thousand thousands shall minister unto him, and ten thousand times ten thousand shall stand before him;" and "the King shall say unto them on his right hand, Come, ye blessed of my Father, inherit the kingdom prepared for you from the foundation of the world."

Jesus Christ has also been anointed as the King of his church. "Yet have I set my King upon my holy hill of Zion." Christ is a king by *personal right.* Jehovah is "King." Christ is Jehovah's "fellow" (Zech. xiii. 7), and therefore he has a Divine right to universal sovereignty. He is king by *donation* from the Father: "All power is given unto me in heaven and in earth:" "Thou hast given him power over all flesh, that he should give eternal life to as many as thou hast given him." "All that the Father giveth me shall come to me." He is king by *purchase:* "Ye are not your own, for ye are bought with a price." He is king by *conquest:* "In righteousness doth he make war."

Of his gracious victories the psalmist writes, "Thine arrows are sharp in the heart of the king's enemies; whereby the people fall under thee." He is king by *voluntary surrender.* His service is perfect freedom. "No man can come unto me, except the Father which hath sent me draw him." Bishop Reynolds says, "As we see human wisdom can so order, moderate, and make use of natural motion, that by it artificial effects shall be produced; as in a clock, the natural motion of the weight and plummet causes the artificial distribution of hours, and minutes; and in a mill, the natural motion of the wind or water causes an artificial effect in grinding the corn: how much more then shall the wisdom of Almighty God be able so to use, incline, and order the wills of men, without destroying either them or their liberty, as that thereby the kingdom of his Son shall be set up amongst them! So that there be still an habitual, radical, fundamental indetermination and indifference unto several ways (unto none of which there can be a compulsion); yet by the *secret*, ineffable, and most sweet operation of the Spirit of grace, opening the eyes, convincing the judgment, persuading the affections, inclining the heart, giving an understanding, quickening and knocking at the conscience, a man shall be swayed unto the obedience of Christ, and shall come unto him as certainly as if he were drawn, and yet as freely as if he were left to himself. For in the calling of men by the word there is a *trahere*, and a *venire*. The Father draweth, and the man cometh, John vi. 44. That notes the efficiency of grace, and this the sweetness of grace. Grace worketh strongly, and therefore God is said to draw; and it worketh sweetly too, and therefore man is said to come."

Satan is an usurper, "the prince of the powers of the air, the spirit that now worketh in the children of disobedience." But Christ is the King of his believing people. Once they, as others, were the slaves of the devil and of sin. When they look back, they acknowledge with humiliation of soul, "O Lord, other lords besides thee have had dominion over us." By grace they have given themselves to the Lord, and have entered into a perpetual covenant with him, that shall never be forgotten. What privileges do they enjoy as the subjects of Jesus! He is their King, and he defends them. His church is his vineyard, purchased with his own blood, and "lest any hurt it, he keeps it night and day." "When the enemy shall come in like a flood, the Spirit of the Lord shall lift up a standard against him." He is their King, and he bestows upon them honourable titles. They are not servants, but friends, yea his children: "Now are we the sons of God." He condescends to call them lambs, for gentleness; doves, for innocence; serpents, for wisdom; and eagles, for spirituality. They are trees, for fruitfulness; and flowers, for fragrance: they are his "peculiar" treasure, jewels of inestimable value. They are the salt of the earth, and the light of the world. "All that see them shall acknowledge them, that they are the seed which the Lord hath blessed." He is their King, and bestows upon them precious gifts—not mere earthly possessions (these are often the solemn trust of the unconverted), but "durable riches," grace here and glory hereafter. It is their highest joy to own him as their Lord. His honour is dear to them. His commandments, so far from being esteemed grievous, are "ways of pleasantness and paths of peace." Never are they so happy as when they hold communion with him, or labour for him. Never does he pour such sweet consolation into their hearts as when they are reproached for his name, or suffer under his afflicting hand. "In keeping his commandments there is great reward."

Christ has a right to be King of every nation,

every tribe, every family, every heart. But it is not so yet; "we see not yet all things put under him." The Christian mourns over the debasement and ignorance of the heathen, the fanaticism and pride of the Mohammedans, the obstinacy and unbelief of the Jews, the inconsistencies and worldliness of nominal disciples, and, above all, the ingratitude and coldness, and remaining corruption of his own heart. With what joy does he anticipate the blessed time when the whole earth shall be the Lord's, and all shall know him from the least unto the greatest! May God hasten it according to his will.

The last question of our Saviour's public ministry was a very solemn one, "What think ye of Christ?" Let us apply this inquiry to ourselves. What do we think of him? Is he our Prophet, our Priest, our King? How do we think of him? With love, gratitude, and adoration? or with coldness, formality, and reserve?

There is a more solemn question still, "What does Christ think of us?" Ah! we may be mistaken in our thoughts of him; he can never be mistaken or deceived in his thoughts of us. "He searcheth the heart; he trieth the reins." His eyes are a flame of fire. "By him actions are weighed." What does Christ think of us? Let each reader pause, and inquire "What does Christ think of me? Now—in the presence of God—in reference to eternity—what am I? Where am I? Whither am I going? 'Search me, O God, and know my heart; try me, and know my thoughts; and see if there be any wicked way in me, and lead me in the way everlasting.'"

"THE SON OF GOD AND THE SON OF MAN."

"Jesus heard that they had cast him out; and when he had found him, he said unto him, Dost thou believe on the Son of God? He answered and said, Who is he, Lord, that I might believe on him? And Jesus said unto him, Thou hast both seen him, and it is he that talketh with thee."—JOHN ix. 35–37.

"When Jesus came into the coasts of Cesarea Philippi, he asked his disciples, saying, Whom do men say that I the Son of man am?"—MATT. xvi. 13.

THE tabernacle in the wilderness was resplendent with the glory of Jesus. Every part of the sacred structure shadowed forth his Deity and his humanity. Its division into the holy and most holy place; its cedar boards covered with golden plates; its earthy floor and its gorgeous canopy; the vessels of the sanctuary; the sacrifices, and the incense, all proclaimed to a spiritual worshipper that the promised Seed, the Son of David, was both the Son of God and the Son of man. From a consideration of some of the proofs of the Messiahship of Jesus, it naturally follows that we meditate upon the mystery of his person. "Without controversy great is the mystery of godliness: God was manifest in the flesh." With holy reverence, therefore, and humble prayer for Divine teaching, let us draw near and contemplate Him, who is both the "root and offspring of David," the "man of sorrows," and the "God of glory."

It was a prominent article in the creed of the ancient Jews, that the Messiah was to be the Son of God. Accordingly Nathanael witnessed a good confession when he said, "Rabbi, thou art the Son of God; thou art the King of Israel." Peter, in the name of the other apostles, said, "Thou art the Christ, the Son of the living God." More fully, and with yet greater assurance of reality in what he said, we find Peter answering the inquiry, "Will ye also go away?" by the emphatic testimony, "Lord, to whom shall we go? thou hast the words of eternal life. And we believe and are sure that thou art that Christ, the Son of the living God." Martha, the sister of Lazarus, said to her Divine Master, "I believe that thou art the Christ, the Son of God, which should come into the world." And when Jesus stood upon his trial, "the high priest answered and said unto him, I adjure thee by the living God that thou tell us whether thou be the Christ, the Son of God. Jesus saith unto him, Thou hast said: nevertheless I say unto you, Hereafter shall ye see the Son of man sitting on the right hand of power, and coming in the clouds of heaven." Christ then claimed the title of the Son of God: "Thou hast said." Nor was this the only occasion. He welcomed and comforted the man to whom he had given sight, and whom, for his confession of the truth, the Pharisees had cast out of the synagogue; and that which was judicially "hidden from the wise and prudent," was revealed unto a babe. "Thou hast both seen him, and it is he," the Son of God, "which talketh with thee." Jesus declared the same truth publicly. When the Jews charged him with blasphemy, for "making himself equal with God," he answered them from their own Scripture: "Is it not written in your law, I said, Ye are gods? If he called them gods, unto whom the word of God came, (and the Scripture cannot be broken;) say ye of him, whom the Father hath sanctified, and sent into the world, Thou blasphemest; because I said, I am the Son of God?"

In what sense are we to understand that Jesus

is "the Son of God?" At the creation we are told that the "morning stars sang together, and all the sons of God shouted for joy;" that is, the holy angels rejoiced in, and adored their glorious Maker. Adam is said to be "the son of God," Luke iii. 38. Believers are called "the sons of God;" but angels are the sons of God by creation; believers are his sons by adoption; Jesus Christ is the Son of God by eternal generation. Angels and men are but creatures: Christ is the Creator of all things. Believers were once strangers and enemies, and they have been reconciled by blood, and adopted by grace into God's family: Jesus Christ was ever with the Father, "rejoicing always before him;" co-equal and co-eternal with him, "the brightness of his glory, and the express image of his person," the only begotten Son of God.

The proofs that Jesus, the Son of God, is equal with the Father—God of God—Light of Light—very God of very God—are clear, strong, and numerous.

Look at the *statements of the Bible.* "In the beginning God created the heaven and the earth." "In the beginning was the Word, and the Word was with God, and the Word was God. The same was in the beginning with God. All things were made by him; and without him was not anything made that was made." "I and my Father are one." "Of whom, as concerning the flesh, Christ came, who is over all, God blessed for ever.—Amen." How convincing is the testimony of the prophets to the Deity and humanity of Jesus! We read in Isaiah: "Unto us a Child is born," mark his human nature: "Unto us a Son is given," mark his Divine nature (compare John iii. 16): "and the government shall be upon his shoulder: and his name shall be called Wonderful, Counsellor, The mighty God, The everlasting Father, The Prince of Peace." Micah says, "Thou, Bethlehem Ephratah, though thou be little among the thousands of Judah, yet out of thee shall he come forth unto me," here is his human nature, "that is to be Ruler in Israel; whose goings forth have been from of old, from everlasting," here is his Divine nature. To quote only one more passage; Jeremiah says, "Behold, the days come, saith the Lord, that I will raise unto David a righteous Branch," here is the human nature of Christ; "and a King shall reign and prosper, and shall execute judgment and justice in the earth. In his days Judah shall be saved, and Israel shall dwell safely: and this is his name whereby he shall be called, THE LORD OUR RIGHTEOUSNESS;" here is his Divine nature.

Consider one remarkable feature in the *miracles* of Jesus, namely, they were performed by *his own, not a derived* power. Moses, Elijah, Elisha, and the apostles wrought miracles by power from heaven. They were instruments of God's power when they wrought miracles, as they were instruments of his wisdom and knowledge when they wrote books of Holy Scripture, and instruments of his grace when they converted souls. But when Jesus wrought miracles, he acted freely and independently, with the authority and majesty of God himself. "Talitha cumi." "Young man, I say unto thee, Arise." "Lazarus, come forth." His miracles, therefore, were proofs of his Deity.

Consider the argument from the *parity of names, attributes*, and *operations*. There are names, attributes, and operations assigned to Jehovah, in the Scripture, which are the property of God alone. If these are assigned to Jesus Christ, it must follow that Jesus Christ is of the same nature with God. On this head, we cannot do better than quote the references of Bishop Beveridge: "The Father is called Jehovah, and so is the Son: Isa. vi. 3; Hos. i. 7. The Father is called God, so is the Son:

John i. 1, 'In the beginning was the Word, and the Word was with God, and the Word was God.' 'With God' as to his person, 'God' himself as to his essence: so John xx. 28; Acts xx. 28; 1 Tim. iii. 16. The Father is Alpha and Omega, the first and the last: Isa. xli. 4; xliv. 6. So is the Son: Rev. i. 8–17. Is the Father eternal? So is the Son: Isa. ix. 6; Rev. i. 8. Is the Father Almighty? So is the Son: Heb. i. 3. Is the Father everywhere? So is the Son: Matt. xviii. 20. Doth the Father know all things? So doth the Son: John xxi. 17. Did the Father make all things? So did the Son: John i. 3. Doth the Father preserve and uphold all things? So doth the Son: Heb. i. 3. Doth the Father forgive sins? So doth the Son: Matt. ix. 6."

Further, without question, Jesus Christ knew the mind of God. It was his meat and his drink to do his Father's will. Would he then give any sanction to idolatry? If I pay religious homage to a creature, I am guilty of idolatry. Hence Peter refused the homage of Cornelius, when "he fell down at his feet, and worshipped him. Peter took him up, saying, Stand up; I myself also am a man." The angel at whose feet John fell, said, "See thou do it not; I am thy fellow-servant, and of thy brethren that have the testimony of Jesus: worship God." The Lord Jesus never declined the worship of man. The leper knelt before him. After the walking upon the sea, and the calming the tempest, the disciples came and worshipped him, saying, "Of a truth thou art the Son of God." The woman of Canaan prayed unto him, "Have mercy on me, O Lord, thou Son of David; my daughter is grievously vexed with a devil." The blind men who were restored to sight offered a similar prayer. Many more instances might be mentioned. Were these acts of adoration ever discouraged in any single instance? If Jesus were only a man, then all these cases were acts of idolatry, and our Lord went about (with reverence we write it) teaching and encouraging idolatry. But what were the words of Jesus himself? "That all men should honour the Son even as they honour the Father." And what was his command immediately before his ascension? "Go ye therefore, and teach all nations, baptizing them in the name of the Father, and of the Son, and of the Holy Ghost." Baptism surely is an act of religious worship. Yet baptism is to be administered in the name of Jesus. If, then, we cannot believe that Jesus, the great teacher sent from God, would institute idolatry, he must be a Divine Being equal in authority, majesty, and glory with the Father and Holy Spirit.

Such are some of the scriptural proofs for the Deity of Jesus Christ. We have referred to this subject in a previous chapter, where we entered at some length into the argument from the title "I am Alpha and Omega, the first and the last."

This doctrine is full of unspeakable consolation and instruction. The love of God in the gift of his Son, and the condescension of Christ in effecting our salvation, are exceedingly magnified, if we in any measure realize the eternal dignity and majesty of the Son of God.

The salvation which Jesus has purchased is a Divine work. It has Divine efficacy and merit. It honours God, and it saves man. The holiest creature could only have done his duty, he could not have merited a righteousness for another. But Jesus is "Jehovah *our* righteousness." Neither could a creature have endured the weight of imputed sin; our own sin is an intolerable burden: "A wounded spirit who can bear?" If Jesus had not been a Divine Being, he would have sunk under the weight of the sins of the world.

As God, Jesus Christ is "able to save to the uttermost." He is able to subdue our enemies conquer temptations for us and in us, hear, answer, and satisfy every prayer of our hearts. In him all fulness dwells. All wisdom, knowledge, grace, and power are treasured up in him for his people.

The Lord Jesus, the Son of God, also calls himself the "Son of man." "Who do men say that I the Son of man am?" "The Son of man came not to be ministered unto, but to minister, and to give his life a ransom for many." "The Son of man is come to seek and to save that which was lost." It is a common observation how often Jesus calls himself the "Son of man," and how very seldom he is called so by others. More than sixty passages might be quoted of the former class, and not six of the latter. Once Daniel speaks of Jesus as the "Son of man." Once Stephen said, "I see the heavens opened, and the Son of man standing on the right hand of God;" and John, in the first chapter of Revelation, says, "Being turned, I saw seven golden candlesticks; and in the midst of the seven candlesticks one like unto the Son of man;" and again, in Rev. xiv. 14:

"And I looked, and behold a white cloud, and upon the cloud one sat like unto the Son of man." It was like him to designate himself the "Son of man," for "he made himself of no reputation." It would not have been like his apostles, to whom he was so precious, and who sought his glory as the one object of their lives, to apply to him, in their ordinary method of speech, a title of humiliation—and it was such, take it how we will. Some simply understand by the title that Jesus was the "Seed of the woman," the promised Son of David. Others look upon it as an expression on his part of his humanity. Dean Trench thinks that he is so called, because he was the only specimen which earth has ever witnessed of man in his high and true estate. Man in ruins cannot be called the true idea of man. You would hardly say of the mounds and morasses of Babylon, and of the excavations of Nineveh, There is Babylon, or There is Nineveh. And of man—sinful, depraved, diseased, and dying man—you can hardly say, There is man. The naturalist would not select as an illustration of an order of creatures, some broken or mutilated thing, but the most perfect that he could find; and so Trench says, that "Christ alone realized the idea of man, the second Adam, who, unlike the first, should maintain his position as the head and representative of the race—the one true and perfect flower which had ever unfolded itself out of the root and stalk of humanity."

The proofs of the human nature of Jesus meet us everywhere in the Gospels. We shall best satisfy our readers, if we again refer to Bishop Beveridge's arrangement of texts on this head. "As the Son of God was begotten of the same substance with God the Father from eternity, so was he conceived of the same substance with us men in time; and therefore is there nothing that belongs to us as men, but what he took upon himself. Have we a body? so had he, Heb. x. 5, 10: have we flesh and blood? so had he, Heb. ii. 14: have we hands and feet? so had he, Luke xxiv. 39: have we a soul? so had he, Matthew xxvi. 38. Are we hungered? so was he, Matthew iv. 2: and weary? so was he, John iv. 6: and heavy and sorrowful? so was he, Mark xiv. 33. Do we grow in stature and knowledge? so did he, Luke ii. 52. Do we die? so did he—he gave up the ghost too, John xix. 30. Thus was he in all things tempted like us, yet without sin,

Hebrews ii. 17; iv. 15. So well may he be called the *man Christ Jesus*, 1 Timothy ii. 5; 1 Corinthians xv. 21: and *Christ Jesus the Son of man*, Matthew xxvi. 2."

How great was the condescension of the Lord Jesus! "Though he was rich, yet for your sakes he became poor, that ye through his poverty might be rich." Jehovah's "fellow" became very man. How wonderful that the Creator should voluntarily abase himself to become a creature; that the only begotten Word of the Father should be "born of a woman;" that he who "upholds all things by the word of his power," should himself be upheld in his mother's arms; that he, in whom all men "live and move, and have their being," should himself draw sustenance from his mother's breast; that the boy in the temple at Jerusalem should himself be the very Wisdom of God, from whom the sages of the law derived their understanding, and their hard questions; that the Teacher, who instructed Nicodemus by night, was himself both on earth and in heaven! "No man hath ascended up to heaven, but he that came down from heaven, even the Son of man which is in heaven." Three wonders meet in that verse of John (chapter i. 10). "He was in the world," observe the condescension of his humanity; "and the world was made by him," mark the glory of his Deity; "and the world knew him not." This is the greatest wonder, that men knew not their Creator, Redeemer, and Lord.

The humanity of Jesus assures us of his deep and tender sympathy: "For he that toucheth you, toucheth the apple of his eye." "We have not an High Priest which cannot be touched with the feeling of our infirmities; but was in all points tempted like as we are, yet without sin." The Lord Jesus passed through the various stages of man's condition, that he might experimentally feel for each and for all. He was emphatically the "man of sorrows." Are we oppressed by poverty? He could say, "Foxes have holes, and the birds of the air have nests; but the Son of man hath not where to lay his head." Are we suffering under agonizing bereavement? He wept at Lazarus's grave. Have we to encounter shame and reproach for him? He endured the "contradiction of sinners against himself." Have we to grapple with spiritual enemies? "He himself hath suffered, being tempted; and he is able to succour them that are tempted." He is the head of his church. We are his members. We are one with him. He is one with us. Most intimate is the sympathy between Jesus and his saints. He is their "all in all," "the chiefest among ten thousand." We are thus encouraged to put all our trust in Jesus Christ, and to commit our way to him, believing that he will perfect his own work in our souls.

"THE BREAD OF LIFE."

"I am that bread of life."—John vi. 48.

Hitherto our attention has been directed to these titles and names of Christ assumed by himself, which we may regard as *personal*, because they set forth his personal attributes, and what he is in himself, in the adorable mystery of his person—God and man in one Christ. We now turn to those titles and names which may be regarded as *descriptive*, rather than as personal, because Christ has, in condescension to our infirmities, been pleased to apply to himself some familiar object as an emblem, descriptive of what he is to us, and of our duty towards him. These descriptive titles are almost entirely peculiar to the writings of John. To him it was permitted to record the more intimate conversations of Christ with his disciples; and to him we are indebted for the beautiful and suggestive titles upon which we now enter, the "Bread of Life," the "Light of the World," the "Good Shepherd," the "Resurrection and the Life," etc.

"I am that bread of life." The Lord Jesus thus applies to himself the celebrated gift of the manna in the wilderness. "Moses gave you not that bread from heaven; but my Father giveth you the true bread from heaven. For the bread of God is he which cometh down from heaven, and giveth life unto the world."

The manna was the gift of God. "God so loved the world, that he gave his only begotten Son." The manna was given freely. No merit could the children of Israel claim. Rather, the merit was the other way. They might have expected fire from heaven, but not food. They were guilty rebels, murmuring in their unbelief, as though God had brought them out of Egypt to die in the wilderness. The plagues of Egypt, the passage through the Red Sea, and the mysterious pillar of cloud which overshadowed and guided them day by day, had not taught them to trust in the Lord Jehovah. When the bread which they had brought with them out of Egypt was spent, they murmured against Moses and against God. How marvellous the patience and the grace of the Most High! God, who is rich in mercy, chose to still the fretful murmurs of his first born with the breast rather than the rod. He bids the heaven supply by its bounty what the earth denied by its barrenness; and, without their toil or sweat, gives them plenty of bread even in a land that was not sown. And has not "God commended his love toward *us*, in that while we were yet sinners, Christ died for us?" The sandy desert was barren and utterly destitute of any sustenance for the numerous host, and God opened for them the treasures of the sky, and gave them corn from heaven, and invited them to partake of angels' food. Earth could provide no Saviour for man: "None can by any means redeem his brother, nor give to God a ransom for him." Christ "saw that there was no man, and wondered that there was no intercessor: therefore his arm brought salvation unto him; and his righteousness, it sustained him." We are told in Numbers xi. 9, that "when the dew fell upon the camp in the night, the manna fell upon it;" and in Exodus xvi. 13, that "the dew lay round about the host." Most abundant was the provision, in the midst of which the congregation of Israel dwelt, and most striking was the "goodness" with which God had prepared a table in the wilderness for his people. The dew was a sovereign gift, which "tarrieth not for man, nor waiteth for the sons of men." At night the manna fell; and dark indeed was the moral night of this world when Jesus was given to tabernacle among us. For more than fifteen hundred years, the Jews had been the favoured depositaries of the oracles of heaven, and yet they rejected the Messiah, and crucified the Lord of glory. Greece and Rome had reached the highest point of fame and civilization; but let the first chapter of Romans testify how ineffectual is intellect without grace to produce virtue, and purity, and happiness here, or to confer a hope of immortality hereafter. Surely, then, it was the "fulness of time" when the Lord Jesus came into the world, if we only regard the darkness of the moral night in which the nations were enshrouded. Jesus is the gift of God. Grace shines throughout it. Mercy to the fallen, grace to the lost; yea, most abundant grace: to be preached to all nations, and to be offered to every creature. The manna lay outside the host. And Christ's arm of mercy encircles the human family. The invitation is as free as the air we breathe, and as extensive as the globe; "Look unto me, and be ye saved, all the ends of the earth."

The manna was to be gathered. The Israelites

had to stoop down, and to put forth their hand, and appropriate portion by portion, if they wished to avoid perishing from hunger in the wilderness. It is not enough for us that Christ has died, and has made a full, perfect, and sufficient satisfaction for the sins of the whole world.* We must come to him. We must appropriate him to our souls by faith.

The manna was to be gathered in the morning. If done at all, the work must be done at the opening dawn. "Remember thy Creator in the days of thy youth." "I love them that love me; and those that seek me early shall find me." "In the morning sow thy seed." Let the First have the first. Some give the dregs of their life to God, and hope to creep into heaven at the eleventh hour. How deep and how foul is the ingratitude of such conduct! Does a youthful eye rest upon this page? Let me invite such an one to taste of true happiness by coming at once to Jesus. Let your opening and expanding powers of mind and

* While the atonement is of infinite sufficiency, it is only efficient in the case of those who penitently and believingly receive it. The writer, evidently, does not teach that Christ made satisfaction for the sins of those who finally perish, otherwise they would have been saved; but that it was so sufficient that the whole world might avail themselves of its benefits.—*Editor of the Board of Publication.*

body be devoted to him. Come to Jesus now, and let Dudley Tyng's dying words be the motto of your daily life, "Stand up for Jesus."

Gather spiritual manna at the morning hour of each day. Imitate the example of Him who "rose a great while before day," that he might enjoy communion with his Father in heaven. Make time for secret morning devotion. "The arrow long retains the first direction of the impelling hand. The vessel rarely loses the savour of its first contents. The day-break blessing is a day-long gain. Let Jesus draw back your morning curtain, and he will sanctify the mid-day labour, and lull you to the night's repose." * If you would be serious, and holy, and useful—if you would walk in the light of the Lord through the day—give the moments of early morning to prayer and reading the word of God. This is the secret of the strength of Christians. General Havelock, whose memory is so fragrant in all the churches of Jesus, set apart two hours for secret devotional exercises before he entered into the public business of each day. Havelock was permitted to relieve Lucknow; and he was called away from the admiration of a grate-

* Archdeacon Law.

ful country to receive the "crown of life," radiant with immortal splendour.

All had to gather the manna. There was an ample supply for all. Some gathered much, others less: "He that gathered much had nothing over, and he that gathered little had no lack." All need to come to Jesus. All are invited to come to him. All who do come, find in him an all-sufficient portion. The manna was parted liberally to all. None are straitened in Jesus Christ: "They shall be abundantly satisfied with the fatness of God's house; and thou shalt make them drink of the river of thy pleasures." The manna was equally distributed among the Israelites. So, all believers, of every sex, of every age, of every nation, strong or weak, eminent or obscure, do equally partake in the common salvation; for all are one in Christ Jesus. The manna was to be gathered day by day, and not to be hoarded. Thus were the Israelites taught to depend upon God for their daily bread, and to beware of covetousness. Manna was not to be gathered on the Sabbath day. Thus did God put honour upon his own day, and thus would he teach us to look forward to that eternal Sabbath, where the means of grace and the ordinances of religion will be laid aside, and where there is no need of the sun, neither of the moon, to shine in the heavenly temple; for the glory of God doth lighten it, and the Lamb is the light thereof.

Having glanced at a few features of the origin and distribution of the manna, let us take some up in the hand of faith, and inquire what it teaches us about Jesus Christ, the "Bread of life."

It was the natural exclamation of the people, when they first saw the manna, "What is this?" They had never seen it before; they had never tasted it; they knew it not. Alas, how many are ignorant of Jesus Christ! Millions have never heard his sweet and blessed name; and millions more have heard his name and his gospel, and yet, in the experience of their hearts, are totally ignorant of him. But when the manna had been tasted, then that which at first was an exclamation of surprise and ignorance, by a slight literal alteration passed into an expression of adoration and gratitude. "Manna," What is it? became "Maneh," a portion — an abundant portion. It is even so with Jesus. For years, we may have been in ignorance and carelessness respecting him. But let our hearts be touched by Divine grace, and let us but come to him, and receive his blessed welcome and his free pardon; let us but enjoy deep and full communion with him, and then our hearts shall acknowledge that Christ is a portion indeed. He is all my salvation, and all my desire.

The manna was "small;"—in appearance, like a little seed. To the eye of sense, it might seem very poor nourishment for an army—too poor, certainly, to be the gift of Heaven. When Jesus "came unto his own, his own received him not." "He was despised and rejected of men." The reputed son of a carpenter of Nazareth was thought too humble to be the Son of David, and the King of the Jews. To the world, Jesus appears but "small." They take no account of him in their political schemes, or in their family arrangements. Self is the great idol. Pleasure, pride, and pelf are the trinity of the world, and the Lord Jesus is dishonoured and cast out; even believers are too often ashamed of him; and the Saviour is wounded in the house of his professed servants and friends.

The manna was "round." The circle was the ancient emblem of eternity. Jesus is the everlasting God, "without beginning of days, or end of years."

The manna was "white." This is the universal idea of purity. Jesus is the Holy One. In him was no sin, neither was guile found in his mouth.

His innocence needed no more argument than the sun needs an argument to prove that he is the brightest luminary in the firmament.

The manna also was "sweet;"—"like honey." Unto them that believe, Jesus Christ is precious. The law of his mouth is dearer to them than thousands of gold and silver. His person, offices, and work are full of sweetness to their souls. When most needed, Jesus Christ is most sweet. When the heart is bleeding with disappointment, he draws near to heal it. When the billows of adversity roll over the spirit of man, he speaks to the wind "Peace," and to the waves "Be still," and "there is a great calm." When sin presses with mountainous weight upon the conscience, his blood, applied by the Holy Spirit, casts the mountain into the sea. Oh, how "sweet" has Jesus proved himself in the moment of temptation, amid the rough sneers of worldly opposition, and in the last, the dying strife! Let us taste and see how gracious the Lord is. It is a matter of personal experience. What is your testimony, reader, to the sweetness of the "Bread of life?"

Before eaten, the manna must be prepared. "It must be gathered, and ground in mills, or beaten in a mortar, and baked in pans, and made into cakes" for the people. Might not all this portray the humiliation and the sufferings through which Jesus passed that he might qualify himself to be our Saviour? Not only must he come from heaven, and take our nature, but he must "bear our sins in his own body on the tree," and endure the judicial fire of the Father's wrath, to purchase our redemption. It is thus also with his people. Affliction is the school of preparation for God's service. The earth must be ploughed up, and the clods broken, if we would reap a plenteous harvest. The olive berries must be crushed, if we would extract the oil. The grapes must be trodden in the wine-press, if they are to yield the "wine which maketh glad the heart of man." The corn must be cut down and laid on the threshing floor, and beaten and winnowed, and ground very small, and kneaded, and baked, if it is to be the staff of man's life: and the believer must suffer, if he is to glorify his Lord, and benefit his fellow-creatures. When he is brought into the very dust, when he is taught his own poverty and wretchedness, then he is in a proper posture to receive good from heaven, and to do good upon earth. When he is most like to his Lord in the patience of discipline, then will he most nearly resemble him in the fruitfulness of sanctification, and devotedness to the will of God.

We may learn much about Christ, the "Bread of life," if we think of the "manna" in contrast with him. Earthly and temporal emblems fall short when they are employed to represent heavenly and eternal realities. No one emblem can do justice to Christ, for all created glory flows from him and centres in him. The "manna" was lifeless; Christ is the living Saviour, with him is the well of life. The "manna" was food for the body; Christ is the true "bread" for the soul. The "manna" could not give, it could only sustain life; Christ is a life-giving, life-sustaining Saviour: "In him we live, and move, and have our being," physically, mentally, spiritually, and eternally. The "manna" could only supply one want: in Christ is all fulness; in him we have "wisdom, and righteousness, and sanctification, and redemption." The "manna" was for one nation only; Christ is the "desire of all nations." The "manna" was given for forty years only, and in one place, the wilderness; Christ has been the refuge and hope of his saints from generation to generation: "Where two or three are gathered together in my name, there am I in the midst of them." "Lo, I am with you alway, even unto the end of the world." Multitudes that partook of the "manna" died in the wilderness; but if we "keep Christ's saying, we shall never taste of death;" to us the death of the body will be the portal to endless life and happiness. The children of Israel wearied of the "manna," and called it "light food;" true believers find increasing joy and treasure in Christ; the longer they live, the richer satisfaction do they experience in studying the wonders of redeeming love. Charles Simeon, on his deathbed, employed himself in dictating the outline of four sermons on Ephesians iii. 18, 19. "So intensely," says his biographer, "were his thoughts fixed on the distribution and illustration of this glorious theme, that he declared he thought no higher honour could be conferred on him, than to be permitted to prepare a set of discourses upon it; and added, 'This is the grandest subject I can conceive of for a course of sermons; I should think a life well spent, even out of heaven, to write and deliver four sermons upon it, in a manner worthy of it.'" Had the Israelites met with other food in the desert, they might have subsisted upon it, as well as upon the manna. Christ is the only Saviour for sinners. "Other foundation can no man lay than that is laid, which is Jesus Christ." "Neither is there salvation in any other: for there is none other name under heaven given among men, whereby we must be saved."

We have remarked, that in the arrangement for gathering the manna, God put special honour upon the Sabbath day; twice as much was to be gathered on the sixth day, that none might be required on the seventh day. The fact that this commandment was given prior to the delivery of the law from Mount Sinai, is one of the many proofs that the Sabbath was a patriarchal and not a Mosaic institution. If the Sabbath were thus made for man, independently of national privilege or peculiarity, then it follows that in its spirit it is binding upon us. The Christian is taught that no unnecessary work is to be done on God's holy day, nothing that may be anticipated on the Saturday, or that may be postponed till the Monday; and, if he be a master or employer, he should afford every possible facility to his dependants to honour the Sabbath.

The arrangement, moreover, that a double portion should fall on the sixth day, and that none should fall on the seventh day, proves that the gift of the manna was not natural, but miraculous. It has been well observed, that the "*natural* manna was never found in the desert, where this fell: where the *natural* manna does fall, it is only in the spring, whereas this fell throughout all the months in the year. The *natural* manna does not melt in the sun, Exodus xvi. 21; does not breed worms, if kept till the morning, verse 20; cannot be ground, so as to make cakes; is medicinal, and therefore cannot be used as food."

Our Saviour's discourse on the "bread of life," in the sixth chapter of John, has been applied by many, who are not Romanists, to the sacrament of the supper of the Lord. We think that Christ would not, by a considerable interval, have thus antedated the institution of that ordinance; and, therefore, that no sacramental theory should be erected upon this chapter, which may not be most clearly demonstrated from other passages of Scripture. Still, in a "spiritual and heavenly manner," the solemn words of Christ may be accommodated to the reception of bread and wine in the holy communion, as well as to every act of a Christian's faith: "Except ye eat the flesh of the Son of man, and drink his blood, ye have no life in you. Whoso eateth my flesh, and drinketh my blood, hath eternal life; and I will raise him up at the last day.

For my flesh is meat indeed, and my blood is drink indeed." In every ordinance that Christ has appointed, as a means of grace, there must be a believing appropriation of him to the soul, even as it was necessary that the manna should be gathered, prepared, and eaten by the Israelites. The mere form of religious service will not profit us anything; there must be the spirit and life, if it is to be acceptable to God, and beneficial to us. Nothing is apparently more simple than that before eating there must be appetite; that in eating there must be actual reception of food; and that after eating there must be digestion, if assimilation and sustenance are to follow. Nothing is so simple as all this, and yet the physiologist will tell us that all this implies one of the most mysterious processes in nature; and so, nothing can be more easily stated upon paper, nothing appears more simple and reasonable when personally realized, than that there must be a sense of need and sinfulness, a belief in the love and power of Jesus, and an habitual abiding in him, and union and communion with him, if the life of God is to flourish in the soul of man. And yet how solemn and how mysterious are all these actings of the Divine Spirit in man! That in secret prayer, while reading the Bible, at the house of God, or at the

Lord's table, in the conscientious fulfilment of daily duty, or in the loving ministrations to the poor of Christ's flock—that in each and all of these means of grace, we are one with Christ, and he is one with us—all this is no less true than it is mysterious; and we learn to analyze diligently our own motives and principles, to labour after reality in our Christian walk, and to offer with all humility and earnestness the prayer of the disciples, "Lord, evermore give us this bread."

"THE LIGHT OF THE WORLD."

"Then spake Jesus again unto them, saying, I am the light of the world: he that followeth me shall not walk in darkness, but shall have the light of life."—JOHN viii. 12.

IT is to be regretted that when the division of the New Testament into chapters and verses was made, the first verse of the eighth chapter of John was separated from the last verse of the seventh chapter; the two verses should have been left in close connection, and then the reader's attention would have been drawn immediately to that which, doubtless, the Holy Spirit intended to illustrate, namely, the homelessness of Jesus: "Every man went unto his own house; Jesus went unto the mount of Olives." The Creator of all things had no home upon his own earth. The world was made by him, and the world knew him not. This is his own testimony, "Foxes have holes, and the birds of the air have nests; but the Son of man hath not where to lay his head."

"And early in the morning" (we read in the eighth chapter and second verse) "he came again into the temple, and all the people came unto him; and he sat down, and taught them." Soon after the great Teacher had commenced his instruction, the case of the "woman taken in adultery" was captiously submitted to his judgment by the Scribes and Pharisees. How strikingly did the "Wisdom of God" frustrate the counsels of his enemies! How clearly did he evince his knowledge of the heart of man, and his sovereignty over conscience! How beautifully did he manifest his compassion for the sinner, and his hatred of sin! "Woman, where are those thine accusers? Hath no man condemned thee? She said, No man, Lord. And Jesus said unto her, Neither do I condemn thee: go, and sin no more." In delicate allusion to this instance of moral darkness and shame; and pointing, probably with his finger, to the bright luminary of heaven, which had only just appeared above the eastern horizon, and was even then dispersing in every direction the clouds of night, and was illuminating the vault of heaven and the face of nature with his glorious beams, Jesus said to his hearers, "I am the light of the world."

Under this emblem, so sublime and significant,

Christ was spoken of by the prophet Malachi: "Unto you that fear my name shall the Sun of righteousness arise with healing in his wings;" and again, the royal psalmist (Psa. lxxxiv. 11), "The Lord God is a sun and shield: the Lord will give grace and glory: no good thing will he withhold from them that walk uprightly."

Let us think for a moment or two on the darkness to which our Saviour referred, and which is driven away by him, the "light of the world." The word "darkness" is used in a fourfold sense. There is the darkness of ignorance. "The dark places of the earth," that is, the places enshrouded in mental and spiritual ignorance, "are full of the habitations of cruelty." There is the darkness of sin: "Men loved darkness rather than light, because their deeds were evil." Ignorance is the parent of crime. The adulterer and the thief, like the "beasts of the forest, creep forth" under the shades of night, to execute their vile designs. There is the darkness of danger and dread. "Are there not twelve hours in the day? If any man walk in the day, he stumbleth not, because he seeth the light of this world: but if a man walk in the night, he stumbleth, because there is no light in him." Night is the time of danger and alarm, when we close our shutters, lock our doors, and draw our bolts and bars, and when we feel, in an especial manner, our need of the protection of our heavenly Father. And there is the darkness of sorrow and misery. To walk in darkness, is to walk in sorrow. To lie down in the "blackness of darkness for ever," is to lie down in hell. The Lord Jesus is the "light of the world." He brought life and immortality to light. Profound indeed was the darkness even of the civilized Roman world at his advent. Cicero may be regarded as a fair specimen of what man could attain to without a revelation from heaven; and yet Cicero was not sure either of the existence of God, or of the immortality of the soul. The Rabbis were designated by our Lord as "blind leaders of the blind." To Nicodemus, the doctrine of the new birth appeared strange; and though the law and the prophets were read in the synagogue every Sabbath day, Paul says that the veil was on the heart of the Jewish nation. Very appropriate, then, was the title which the "Teacher sent from God" assumed to himself, "I am the light of the world." Through succeeding ages, wherever the gospel has been freely and fully proclaimed, there has the light of truth, religion, civilization, and science sprung up. Modern Europe owes all her mental superiority over the nations of the earth to the gospel. And in our own day, Christ, the "light of the world," has illuminated the tribes of the Red Indians, the natives of New Zealand, the islands of the Pacific, and many heathen nations with the "brightness of his rising." We need not stay to show the rich blessings which follow in the train of the gospel. The light of Christian knowledge is succeeded in ten thousand instances by the light of Christian virtue and holiness. "The Son of God was manifested, that he might destroy the works of the devil." He saves all who truly believe in him, from the guilt, the power, and the condemnation of sin. He is the consolation of Israel, and the "Prince of peace." He despoils death of its sting, and the grave of its victory. He "opens the kingdom of heaven to all believers." In every point of view, therefore, darkness yields at his appearing. Christ is the "true Light, which lighteth every man that cometh into the world."

We proceed to consider the instruction from the character and offices of the Saviour which the emblem suggests.

There is but one sun in our planetary system, and throughout the ample extent of this system the sun is the one source of light. Towards the sun each planet with its moons and satellites, turns its every portion of surface to receive light; and round the sun, as the great centre of attraction, each planet journeys in its fixed order of march, and thus enjoys innumerable blessings from him. There is but one Saviour for sinners; one light for the moral and spiritual world. Without Jesus every human soul is wrapt in darkness. From him believers obtain all the blessings of grace and glory. To him do they daily look for light, and in obedience to him they journey forward, each in his own orbit, appointed by infinite, unerring wisdom and love.

The sun is the brightest luminary in the firmament. In his splendour the moon and the stars pale their feebler radiance. The Lord Jesus "in all things must have the pre-eminence." He is "the chiefest among ten thousand." When his light and love enter into and fill the soul, all inferior lights of worldly pleasure are extinguished. The man of the world walks by taper-light; the Christian walks by sun-light. What are ten thousand thousand tapers compared to the sun?

The sun is of prodigious magnitude. Our earth appears to us a huge rotundity; it is 25,000 miles round, and has a surface of 200,000,000 square miles. But what is our earth to the sun? About one to a million. The highest mountain bears the proportion to the whole earth of a grain of sand lying upon an eighteen-inch globe. What then must a mountain be to the sun? And if a mountain be to the sun so minute a speck, what must *man* be who, on a plane surface, can only see two miles and a half on every side of him? What must the lower animals be? What the tiny flower amid the Alpine snow? What the insects that float upon the sunbeam? Yet the light that streams from the sun travels 97,000,000 miles before it reaches us, and, in order, gladdens and enlightens all. The loftiest mountains and the most secluded valley, the lordly palace and the humble cot, the monarch on the throne and the beggar in the dungeon, are visited and cheered by his beams. Think of the magnitude of the sun, and the minuteness of his operations; the distance of the sun, and yet his nearness to every one of us. If the sun be so great, what must its Divine Creator, "the Sun of righteousness," be! On a fine winter's night the naked eye can discern a thousand stars, some of them larger than our sun; and each of these, it is believed by astronomers, the sun of a separate system, the sovereign luminary of its own territory.

Through a powerful glass 80,000,000 of these are brought to view. How sublime, then, the amplitude of His dominion who "filleth heaven and earth!" How unspeakably magnificent the power of the Lord Jesus! How infinite the distance between the Creator Saviour and man whom he has loved! How wonderful that he who thus has built all things, and has peopled immensity with the creatures of his hands, should humble himself to visit our planet, and to take the nature of rebel man, and in that nature effect an atonement upon the cross by which the rebel is pardoned, accepted, and saved; and the principalities and powers in heavenly places, perhaps the intelligent beings in other planets, and in other systems, are instructed in the manifold wisdom of God! Nor is this all: one main object wherefore the Son of God abased himself and made this stupendous sacrifice, was that he might purchase from his Father for men the gift of the Holy Spirit. In this manner the heart of man is made the temple of God. The light of the Sun of righteousness thus shines, not only upon, but in man, without any respect of persons. "For the same Lord over all is rich unto all that call upon him." Surely we may say with David, "Who is like unto the Lord our God, who dwelleth on high, who humbleth himself to behold the things that are in heaven, and in the earth? He raiseth up the poor out of the dust, and lifteth the needy out of the dunghill; that he may set him with princes, even with the princes of his people." "Pray," said an infidel to an honest countryman on his way to church, "whither are you going?" "To church." "What for?" "To worship God." "Can you tell me whether your God is a little God, or a great God?" "He is both," replied the countryman. "Both! how so?" rejoined the infidel. "He is so great that he fills heaven and earth, and he is so small that he can dwell in my poor heart." "Wisdom is justified of her children."

The sun is eminently beautiful in himself, and he confers beauty upon every object. This beauty is simple and yet composite. Pure white light, when refracted and reflected by the drops of rain, or analyzed by a prism, is proved to consist of seven colours; the most opposite colours are combined in the formation of pencils of light. Even so, in the Lord Jesus, there is a combination of excellences. He is "all fair," and his purity and holiness are "without spot and blemish." The sevenfold gifts of the Spirit "rest upon him: the spirit of wisdom and understanding, the spirit of counsel and might, the spirit of knowledge, and of the fear of the Lord."

"As is his majesty, so is his mercy." The Lion of the tribe of Judah is the "Lamb of God which taketh away the sin of the world." The sovereign of all is the servant of all. The beauties of the landscape are derived from the sun; the variety of hues that meet the eye are painted by him. The clouds, the ocean, the fields, the hedges, the hills, the streams, the trees, with their rich fruit and luxuriant foliage, the plants, with their exquisitely tinted flowers, all reflect, and distribute far and wide the gladdening smile of the sun which falls upon them. If it be true that colour differs according to texture, different textures absorbing and reflecting different portions of colour from the solar rays, then we see how the Creator of these fabrics and of the light which paints them, has ordered each and all, so that each shall be beautiful in itself, each shall contribute to the beauty of the whole landscape, and all redound to the glory of God. It is thus in the system of grace. The disciples of Jesus are "black, but comely." In themselves they are black, polluted, and defiled; but in Jesus they are comely; "their beauty is perfect, through the comeliness which the Lord Jesus has put upon them." Their dispositions and characters vary according to the gifts of God. The grace of Jesus makes them all beautiful in holiness, and radiant with the smile and favour of their Beloved. In position, talents, circumstances, and measure of influence, they vary. One is a servant, another a master; one, as the herald of the cross, preaches to thousands; another, in the service of the word, visits the sorrowful and the sick in the abodes of destitution and dens of wickedness; all the saints of Jesus shine in his light, and they glorify God "in their body and in their spirit, which are his."

The sun is eminently beneficial. Light, heat, and fertility flow from his beams. Blot the sun from the firmament, and our earth would quickly become the region of mourning, lamentation, and woe. How pathetically does Milton lament over his blindness:—

> "With the year
> Seasons return; but not to me returns
> Day, or the sweet approach of even or morn,
> Or sight of vernal bloom, or summer's rose,
> Or flocks, or herds, or human face divine;
> But cloud instead, and ever-during dark,
> Surround me, from the cheerful ways of men
> Cut off, and for the book of knowledge fair
> Presented with an universal blank
> Of Nature's works, to me expunged and razed,
> And wisdom, at one entrance, quite shut out."

Milton had many alleviations in his calamity; he had friends who comforted him, and daughters who read to him. For years he had enjoyed the blessing of sight, and his vigorous memory could people his imagination with the scenes of former days, and portray upon his mental vision a thousand objects in nature and art which once it was his happiness to behold. If there were no sun, what would be the benefit of sight? This world, beautiful even in its fall, would be a gloomy prison-house of despair and death. In what a deplorable state would our souls be without Jesus! Apart from him, we should have no spiritual knowledge, no happy love to God or to man for his sake, no holy conformity to his image, and no fruitfulness to his glory. Without Jesus we can do nothing, in repentance, or in faith, or in obedience, or in patience. In him is the light of life, and without him there would be no holiness or happiness, either in earth or in heaven.

We may gather some sweet thoughts of Jesus, from what are called the laws of light, or the modes of its operation. Is the sun an inexhaustible fountain of light? In Jesus there is an infinite fulness of grace for all his redeemed people. Does light travel with amazing rapidity? How swiftly do the thoughts of the heart of Jesus flow out toward his servants, "thoughts of peace, and not of evil, to give you an expected end!" "Before they call, I will answer." Does light travel only in straight lines? The Lord Jesus is a holy Saviour; his eyes look straight before him in the prosecution of his Father's purposes. Is the angle of reflection always equal to the angle of incidence? The Christian knows that in proportion as he receives grace from Jesus, so will he act grace for Jesus; and that the light which he receives from heaven, he will find it his honour and his happiness to reflect upon earth. Is light, like heat and electricity, a radiant force? It follows, that a small approximation to its centre brings a great increase of influence. It is thus in our relation to Jesus: he is the centre of spiritual influence and power. Our prayers, the goings forth of our hearts to him, how weak, how imperfect are they; and how small is the real approach which we make to him; and how great is his mercy and love to us! The more closely we walk with him, the more shall we realize his grace to our souls.

Again, reflect upon what is popularly called the rising of the sun. See how he climbs higher and higher in his beneficent journey, "as a bridegroom coming out of his chamber, and rejoiceth as a strong man to run a race." Behold a striking emblem of the rising of the Sun of righteousness. Mark the first streak of the light of hope and salvation for our fallen humanity in the promise given in Eden—"the Seed of the woman shall bruise the serpent's head." See how another broad streak was added in the prophecy of "Enoch, the seventh from Adam—Behold, the Lord cometh with ten thousand of his saints." Look at the deliverance of Noah and his family from perishing by water, a prophecy by fact of the salvation wrought out by Christ Jesus. See how the promise to Abraham was renewed to Isaac, and confirmed and extended to Jacob, "In thy seed shall all the families of the earth be blessed." How high, comparatively, had the sun risen, when the dying patriarch said, "The sceptre shall not depart from Judah, nor a lawgiver from between his feet, until Shiloh come; and unto him shall the gathering of the people be;" and when he could calmly lie down in the grave in peace and hope with the prayer, "I have waited for thy salvation, O Lord!" See how fully, though amid the shadows of an external ritual, the gospel was preached by Moses. What light would rise in the mind of many a devout Israelite when he contemplated the pillar of cloud and of fire; when he gathered his daily portion of manna; when he drank water from the smitten rock; when he was healed by looking upon the serpent of brass; and when he saw the tabernacle of witness, and took his own part in its solemn services! And when the people of the Lord were settled in their inheritances in the promised land, mark how prophecy took up the wondrous tale.

See how the light of the knowledge of the Saviour extended from age to age, from Samuel to Malachi, with increasing distinctness: his tribe—his family—his mother—his birthplace—his miracles—his doctrines—his crucifixion—his resurrection, and the "glory that should follow." How gradually was all this foretold! With what rapture of hope did the latter prophets sing of the coming Deliverer! And with Malachi, how did prophecy expire, as it were, with the gospel on its tongue, "Unto you that fear my name shall the Sun of righteousness arise with healing in his wings.—Behold, I will send you Elijah the prophet before the coming of the great and dreadful day of the Lord!" At length, in the "fulness of time," the promised Saviour was born; the true Light shone upon the world. The words of Isaiah were accomplished, "The people that walked in darkness have seen a great light: they that dwell in the land of the shadow of death, upon them hath the light shined;" and Christ himself could say, "I am the light of the world." Heathens are in the darkness of night; the Jews, who still reject their Messiah, are in twilight; Christians enjoy the noontide brightness of the Sun of righteousness. How exalted are our privileges! how grave and solemn are our responsibilities!

When the gospel is first preached to a nation or a community, Jesus rises upon that nation with healing in his wings. It is thus also, when the first entry of the gospel is made by the Holy Spirit into man's heart. Whilst unconverted, he "sat in darkness," he was satisfied in worse than Egyptian bondage; but when he is enlightened, the Spirit speaks with power in his soul, "Awake, thou that sleepest, and arise from the dead, and Christ shall give thee light." How great, how marvellous is the change! Once darkness, he is now light in the Lord. All things are become new. He sees everything in a new light. He is like a man, who for years has been immured in a dungeon, and who has been brought unexpectedly into light and liberty. He is like a man born blind, to whom all the wonders of nature are suddenly opened. When Christ rises upon a man's heart, light, and hope, and peace, and gladness rise, and he is transported with a "joy unspeakable and full of glory." What does the Scripture say of the course of such a convert? "He shall go out with joy, and be led forth with peace; the mountains and the hills shall break forth into singing, and all the trees of the field shall clap their hands." He grows in grace and in knowledge. He waxes stronger and stronger. "Light is sown for the righteous, and gladness for the upright in heart." "The path of the just is as the shining light, that shineth more and more unto the perfect day."

In conclusion, should we not inquire, what do we know experimentally of this great change? Have we been brought out of darkness into light, and from the power of Satan unto God? Let us not rest till this important question has received a satisfactory answer.

If we are the children of light and of the day, let us learn to walk, not as others who are still in darkness, but in obedience to our dear Master and only Saviour Christ Jesus. "Let us put on the armour of light." "Let us walk honestly, as in the day." Let us "shine as lights in the world; holding forth the word of life." Let us in our conversation, influence, and example, at all times, and in all circumstances, remember "whose we are and whom we serve," and let the joyful object of our life be to spread the light of life to all around us.

Great things are in store for us if we hold fast our steadfastness firm unto the end. Glorious is the prospect before us: "If children, then heirs, heirs of God, and joint heirs with Christ." If faithful unto death, we shall receive the crown of life. By grace we have a title to "an inheritance incorruptible, and undefiled, and that fadeth not away." There are greater promises than these. "They that be wise shall shine as the brightness of the firmament; and they that turn many to righteousness as the stars for ever and ever." Can there anything higher be added from the volume of inspiration? Yes, for the Saviour has promised that "the righteous shall shine forth as the sun in the kingdom of their Father."

"THE DOOR."

"I am the door: by me if any man enter in, he shall be saved, and shall go in and out, and find pasture."—JOHN x. 9.

How familiar is this representation which Jesus Christ gives of himself: "I am the door!" Plainly it is a metaphor or emblem, by which he intended to reprove the Scribes and Pharisees, and to instruct us. The Roman Catholics, by taking literally what was intended figuratively, have built up the monstrous doctrine of transubstantiation. When our Saviour instituted the sacrament of the supper, he took bread, and when he had given thanks, he brake it, and gave it to his disciples, saying, Take, eat, this is my body which is given for you: do this in remembrance of me. Likewise after supper he took the cup; and when he had given thanks, he gave it to them, saying, Drink ye all of this; for this is my blood of the New Testament, which is shed for you, and for many, for the remission of sins: do this, as oft as ye drink it, in remembrance of me. Because Jesus said, This is my body, and this is my blood, the Romanists teach that after the consecration of the elements by the priest, the bread and wine are changed into the very body and blood of the Lord. And, say they, nothing can be more plain, for we only take Jesus at his word, for he says, This is my body, and this is my blood. We may answer, that if one emblem is to be taken in this literal manner, another must be taken in the like manner. Jesus said, "I am the vine." Is he then literally a tree? He said, "I am the light of the world." Is he then literally the sun? He said, "I am the door." Is he then the timber and nails of which the door is made? Everybody must see the folly of such a method of interpretation. And, therefore, we are to take these emblems figuratively. The bread and wine represent his body broken, and his blood poured out for sinners; and eating the bread and drinking the wine at his table represent our union and communion with Jesus, and with each other, as his true people. The vine represents him as the source of all our fruitfulness; the sun, as the fountain of innumerable blessings; and the door teaches us, in a lively manner, many lessons about our Lord, as the Mediator between God and man.

"I am the door." A door is a medium of passage. By the door we leave the house, and go forth into the world; by it, others come from without and hold intercourse with us. Jesus Christ is the door to God. "There is one God, and one Mediator between God and men, the man Christ Jesus." Christ is the "Daysman," the peace-maker who reconciles sinners to God, and God to sinners. Therefore he says, "I am the way; no man cometh unto the Father, but by me." And Paul writes, "Being justified by faith, we have peace with God through our Lord Jesus Christ; by whom also we have access by faith into this grace wherein we stand, and rejoice in hope of the glory of God." And again, "Through him we both (Jews and Gentiles) have access by one Spirit unto the Father."

When Jacob left his home as a fugitive, the first night he stopped at Beersheba: alone in the wilderness, he lay down; the ground his bed, the stone his pillow, and the heavens his canopy. It was the season of his distress. Probably he prayed with strong crying and tears, and bitterly lamented his deceitful conduct to his aged father, from whom he was then an exile. The Lord "answered him in the day of his distress." His very sorrow made him sleep, and as he slept, "he dreamed, and, behold, a ladder set up on the earth, and the top of it reached to heaven: and, behold, the angels of God ascending and descending on it. And, behold, the Lord stood above it," and spoke to him words of consolation and encouragement, "I am with thee, and will keep thee in all places whither thou goest, and will bring thee again into this land; for I will not leave thee, until I have done that which I have spoken to thee of." What an apt illustration is this of the mediation of Christ! He is the ladder between earth and heaven, between man and God. By him, the penitent sinner's prayer ascends to heaven; and through him, and for his sake, an answer of peace and forgiveness descends into the soul.

The tabernacle in the wilderness was surrounded by a court. Into this court you entered by a veil of fine linen, curiously wrought with blue, purple, and scarlet. By a similar veil, you entered into the holy place, and into the most holy place. In all these cases, the veil was exactly similar. Through Christ, we enter into the outward and visible church; through him, by his mediation, grace, and Spirit, we are admitted into his true church on earth; and through him, when the work of grace is completed, we are admitted into the holiest, even into heaven itself. Nor is this a fancy. The apostle says, "Having, therefore, brethren, boldness to enter into the holiest by the blood of Jesus, by a new and living way, which he hath consecrated for us, through the veil, that is to say, his flesh; and having an High Priest over the house of God; let us draw near with a true heart in full assurance of faith, having our hearts sprinkled from an evil conscience, and our bodies washed with pure water." Jesus Christ is our "door," our way of access to God.

"I am the door of the sheep." The true sheep of Christ, his "chosen, called, and faithful" people, enter by him, the door. They hear his voice, and by grace they obey it. They appropriate the promises of Jesus to their souls; this is the mark of real Christians, true sheep. Many hear of Christ; few obey, and make use of him. Medicine, not taken, cannot cure. Food, not eaten, cannot nourish. Jesus Christ, not applied by faith, not entered through, as the door, cannot save. The true sheep are those who have been reclaimed from their wanderings, and brought by Christ to God. Once far off, they are made nigh by the blood of Jesus. Once enemies and strangers, they are now his servants, his friends, and his children.

By the door is intended the mode of entrance into the fold. The fold was a plot of ground parted off and strongly enclosed, in order that the sheep might be protected against "thieves and robbers," or wolves and wild beasts. The church of Christ is separated by grace from the world; it is in the world, but not of the world. It is under the peculiar protection of the Almighty. "The gates of hell shall not prevail against it." Jehovah is its keeper; "lest any hurt it, he watches over it night and day." The houses in the East consist of a set of sleeping rooms opening into a quadrangular space, in the centre of which, perhaps, a tree affords its delightful shade, or a sparkling fountain its cool and exhilarating beverage. Here, the inmates meet for conversation; here, the ordinary business of life is transacted; and here, in some instances, for greater protection, the sheep are enfolded at night. To such a house, the entrance is by a low, narrow,* unobtrusive, and substantial door let into

* Dr. Kitto gives the following interesting illustration of Prov. xvii. 19. "He that exalteth his gate seeketh destruction:"—"This is literally true at the present day in the East; but whether this literal interpretation be that which the sacred writer had in view, it may be difficult to determine. It will be remembered that the Oriental houses do not front the street,

an archway in the wall, towards the street; and near it the porter resides. In allusion, probably, to this arrangement, Christ calls himself the Door.

---

but that the entrance from thence leads to a court, in which, or in another beyond it, the front of the main building appears. Hence little indication can be gathered in the street concerning the probable character of the interior building, or the rank or wealth of its inmates, from the appearance of the gate. Aware of this, and aware also that to excite the cupidity of the ruling powers by any indication of wealth is to seek destruction, the wealthiest persons are careful, among other precautions, that their gate shall not betray them, by being less low or mean than the gates of their neighbours. In going through a street, the doors are almost invariably of the most beggarly description—very low; and, although strong, formed of rough, unpainted wood; and on visiting persons whom he may know to be wealthy, the traveller is surprised to be conducted to a gate which, in his own country, he would consider unworthy of a stable or an outhouse, and which but ill prepares him for the splendour and luxury which he may probably find when he reaches the interior. In the city of Bagdad, the only exalted gate to a private residence which the writer recollects to have seen, belonged to the house of a Moslem of large wealth, and of so much influence in the city as, he thought, might allow him to display it freely. He was mistaken. One day, when riding through the street in which he lived, he was dragged from his horse, near our door, and put to death on the spot, by order of the pasha, who immediately took possession of all his property."

The master of the house was also the owner of the sheep. Christ is our Master and Owner. He calls himself the Shepherd and the Door. We are now particularly to contemplate him as the Door. Was the door of an Eastern residence *low*, so that you must stoop at entering? Christ is a door, not for the proud, but for the poor and contrite in spirit.

The question was once asked, Which is the first step to heaven? The answer was "humility;" which is the second step?—"humility;" and the third step?—"humility." Every step towards heaven must be taken in humility. When we first come to Christ, we must come in humility; as we walk daily with him, we must walk in humility; and when we yield our souls to him in death, we must do so in humility, trusting alone in his most precious merits and his everlasting love. Was the door *narrow?* So, if we would enter by Christ upon the way of life, we must leave our worldliness behind. The door can admit us, but not our sins or our lusts; these must be renounced finally and for ever. "Strait is the gate, and narrow is the way, which leadeth unto life; and few there be that find it." Was the door *humble* and unpretending, so that no idea of the wealth of the owner could be gathered from the appearance of the gate towards the street? When the Lord Jesus, the proprietor of all things, came into this world, "he humbled himself, and made himself of no reputation;" he was "meek and lowly in heart." Who would have imagined that the holy child in the temple was the "Wisdom of God?" or that the carpenter of Nazareth was the Divine Architect of the universe? or that the crucified One was the beloved of the Father, "the brightness of his glory, and the express image of his person;" the "heir of all things," to whom all power was given in heaven and earth? Was the door *solid* and massive? and did it present a substantial hindrance to an invading foe? Jesus Christ is a mighty Redeemer, "able to save them to the uttermost that come unto God by him." "He that toucheth you toucheth the apple of his eye." The enemy must destroy him before he can prevail to destroy his sheep. Take an illustration drawn by the pencil of inspiration: "As an eagle stirreth up her nest, fluttereth over her young, spreadeth abroad her wings, taketh them, beareth them on her wings; so the Lord alone did lead him, and there was no strange god with him."

Unless we enter by the door, we can have no knowledge of the wealth of the house, nor of the character of the owner. We have no real knowledge of God except we draw near unto him through his Son, Jesus Christ. "No man hath seen God at any time; the only begotten Son, which is in the bosom of the Father, he hath declared him."

How great are the blessings which Christ promises to those who "enter by him!" "By me, if any man enter in, he shall be saved." The poor wandering sheep brought into the fold is safe and happy. Believers in Jesus are saved with an "everlasting salvation." They are "filled with joy and peace in believing." They are washed in the blood of Christ, they are clothed in the righteousness of Christ, they are freely and fully justified through the merits of Christ, and they are progressively sanctified by the Spirit of Christ. Hooker well remarks of this glorious salvation, "There is a threefold righteousness for believers; there is a justifying righteousness, which is perfect but not inherent; there is a sanctifying righteousness, which is inherent but not perfect; and there will be a glorifying righteousness in the world to come, which is both perfect and inherent."

Liberty, holy, gracious liberty, is also secured in the promise, "He shall go in and out." Always to be in the fold would be imprisonment. Always to be out of the fold would be banishment. Christ's sheep have liberty. The truth has made them "free." They are led forth by their compassionate Shepherd into pasture. He leads them into the treasures of his word, and feeds them with the plenteousness of God's house. He brings them into the fold, and his "banner over them is love." Their Shepherd is ever with them. He will never fail nor forsake them. Their communion with him is free and unrestrained; they come with boldness to the throne of grace. They pour out their hearts before him, and he entrusts the secrets of his covenant and his dealings to them. How pleasing is the testimony of one of the sheep, "The Lord is my Shepherd; I shall not want! He maketh me to lie down in green pastures: he leadeth me beside the still waters. He restoreth my soul: he leadeth me in the paths of righteousness for his name's sake. Yea, though I walk through the valley of the shadow of death, I will fear no evil: for thou art with me; thy rod and thy staff they comfort me."

If we found a door always shut against us, we should leave off trying to effect an entrance. What an unspeakable mercy it is that over the door to present pardon, peace, and holiness, and to everlasting felicity, there is this inscription, "Knock, and it shall be opened unto you." Blessed is he that knocks at mercy's door; for Christ says, "Him that cometh to me, I will in no wise cast out." We may be poor, sorrowful, and unworthy; we may feel (yea, we ought to feel) as if we were beggars at the throne of grace. "The Son of man is come to seek and to save that which was lost." The voice of tender invitation is to "the sons of men," Prov. viii. 4. None are excluded but those who exclude themselves. Though we have to knock again and again, though our wants are so numerous, and our necessities so pressing, yet Christ is never wearied with our prayers. He is ever more ready to hear than we are ready to pray; and he is wont to give more than we can desire or deserve. And should not our own successful experience stimulate us to encourage and invite others to apply to him for his blessing? Christ will not be displeased, for he is rich unto all that call upon him, and rejoices over a repenting sinner with "joy and singing." Christ is then an open door to penitent believers. "The Spirit and the bride say, Come. And let him that heareth say, Come. And let him that is athirst come. And whosoever will, let him take of the water of life freely."

Grace, however, has its time and season. The longest day has an end. The brightest sun will set. God's patience is great with man; but patience will have her "perfect work." His wrath is slow to rise; but when once it is kindled, all the rivers of the south cannot quench it. "Now is the accepted time; behold, now is the day of salvation." Now, the door of mercy may be entered. Now, God is waiting to be gracious. There is a time when conscience speaks, when providences allure or alarm, when the Holy Ghost pleads, when the offers of grace are made, and when the door may be opened by faith and prayer. But, "when once the Master of the house is risen up, and hath shut to the door, and ye begin to stand without, and to knock at the door, saying, Lord, Lord, open unto us; he shall answer and say unto you, I know you not whence ye are."

Noah preached to the sinners of the old world for a hundred and twenty years, all the time the ark was building. There was then a double testimony from God; but they were proof against every admonition, dead to every sound. They ate, they drank, they bought, they sold, they planted, they builded; and in their folly they thought that all things would continue the same as from the beginning of the creation; they believed not in God, and treated the Most High as if he were a liar like unto themselves. The appointed time came. The ark was completed, and stored with all kind of provision. The creatures had all entered and taken their allotted places. Noah and his family embarked in that huge, strange vessel, and the sacred historian adds, "The Lord shut him in." The door that shut *in* Noah and his family, shut *out* the ungodly and the impenitent. Even thus will it be when the "Son of man is revealed." The door of mercy will then be *shut*. When the last elect soul shall be converted and saved, then shall the end come; then shall the flood of fire sweep over a guilty world; then shall it be too late to cry for mercy when it is the time of justice. Oh terrible voice of most just judgment, which shall be pronounced upon them, when it shall be said unto them, "Depart, ye cursed, into everlasting fire, prepared for the devil and his angels!"

In the parable of the ten virgins our Lord says, "They that were ready went in with him to the marriage: and the door was shut." Solemn words! —"the door was shut." They that were ready were safe and happy; but those who were not ready, who had no oil in their vessels, no grace in their hearts, were shut out, and that sorrowful word fell upon their ear, "Depart."

To every individual the door is shut at death.

While there is life there is hope. At death the portion of each is unalterably fixed. As the tree falls, so it lies. As death leaves a man, so will judgment find him—saved by grace, or lost by sin. Death may come gradually. Weeks of languishing may be appointed. Pin by pin the tabernacle may be taken down. A long season may be granted for personal preparation, or for giving a testimony for Christ to those around us. But the door will be shut at last, and the soul will be launched into eternity. Death may summon us in a moment. We know not what a day may bring forth. Like the grass, we may be cut down: "In the morning it flourisheth, and groweth up; in the evening it is cut down, and withereth." Spencer Thornton, the faithful minister of Wendover, rich in faith and good works, was walking in London, when the Lord called him from his work to his reward; he suddenly dropped, fell on the pavement, and the vital spark was gone:—

"They looked—he was dead;
His spirit had fled:
The soul, undressed
From her mortal vest,
Had stepped in her car of heavenly fire;

And proved how bright
Were the realms of light,
Bursting at once upon the sight."

To him sudden death was sudden glory. It is not so with all: many a worldly man has been cut down at a banquet; many with a lie or an oath upon their lips; many in the very act of sin, the rebel hand lifted up against God, and then struck down for ever.

What shall we learn from these considerations? Let us watch and pray. Let us use all "diligence to make onr calling and election sure." Let us arise and go to our Father. Let us henceforth determine, in a strength not our own, with full purpose of heart to cleave to the Lord. "Behold, I stand at the door, and knock: if any man hear my voice, and open the door, I will come in to him, and will sup with him, and he with me."

"THE GOOD SHEPHERD."

"I am the good Shepherd: the good Shepherd giveth his life for the sheep."—JOHN x. 11.

THE character of a shepherd is frequently given in Scripture to our blessed Lord. He says of himself, "I am the good Shepherd: the good Shepherd giveth his life for the sheep. I am the good Shepherd, and know my sheep, and am known of mine. As the Father knoweth me, even so know I the Father: and I lay down my life for the sheep. And other sheep I have which are not of this fold: them also I must bring, and they shall hear my voice; and there shall be one fold and one Shepherd." Peter calls him "the chief Shepherd," 1 Pet. v. 4; and the "Shepherd and Bishop of our souls," 1 Pet. ii. 25. Paul calls him "the great Shepherd of the sheep," Heb. xiii. 20. Isaiah speaks of him as Jehovah God: "Behold, the Lord God will come with strong hand, and his arm shall rule for him; behold, his reward is with him, and his work before him. He shall feed his flock like a shepherd: he shall gather the lambs with his arm, and carry them in his bosom, and shall gently lead those that are with young." What blessed consolation is this to the tried and tempted believer! He does not lean upon an arm of flesh, but upon the living and eternal God. He has a Shepherd who combines the most unlimited power with the most tender sympathy: by faith he can rejoice in tribulation, and smile even in conflict, for he can argue from the strongest premises to the strongest consolation, "Jehovah is my Shepherd: *therefore* can I lack nothing." Whatever office the Lord Jesus sustains to his people, they bear a corresponding relation to him. Is he their Head? they are his members. Is he their Foundation? they are lively stones built upon him. Is he the Vine? they are the branches. Is he their Shepherd? then it follows that they are his sheep.

Let us meditate on the dealings of the Lord Jesus with his chosen, called, and faithful people, in their state of nature, of grace, and of glory.

View the sheep in their *natural* state. They were fallen and guilty; in want and danger; under a sentence of condemnation, and ready to perish. "All we like sheep have gone astray; we have turned every one to his own way." We have not the slightest claim or merit in the sight of a holy God: our very righteousnesses are no better than filthy rags. "If we should keep the whole law, and yet offend in one point, we are guilty of all." If we commit but one sin, we are sinners; and if that one sin be unrepented of, and if it be not washed out in the blood of Christ, that one sin is mighty enough to sink our souls into eternal ruin. The air we breathe surrounds us, and inhabits us: it pervades the depths of ocean; it may be exhausted from the pores of vegetables, and the substance of the hardest metals. It is thus with sin; it insinuates itself into the most secret recesses of all our hearts, and permeates every action of our lives. If we are out of Christ, from day to day we are treasuring up "wrath against the day of wrath."

The good Shepherd came to "seek and to save that which was lost." Nothing but goodness and free grace could have induced him to do this. There was no authority which could compel him, and no application on our part which could incline him. He knew perfectly what it would cost him—even tears, and agony, and blood. But he did not shrink back: on the contrary, he longed for the accomplishment of his work with inexpressible eagerness. "I have a baptism to be baptized with; and how am I straitened till it be accomplished!" Nor was this all. After he had redeemed them by his death, he had to search for his sheep, and to find them in their wanderings, and to bring them to his fold. All mankind are his sheep by the right of creation and supreme sovereignty; but out of the mass of mankind there are those whom he calls peculiarly his own, because they were GIVEN to him by his Father before the foundation of the world. Hence, he says, "As thou hast given him power over all flesh, that he should give eternal life to as many as thou hast given him." If none had been given to Christ from all eternity, none would have given themselves to him in time: if Christ had not loved and chosen them, they would never have loved and chosen him.

How gracious is the Shepherd to his little flock, to whom it is the Father's good pleasure to give the kingdom! "He leaves the ninety and nine, and goeth into the mountains, and seeketh that which is gone astray." And when he has found it, does he complain of his privations, and fatigues, and sufferings? does he drive it into the fold, or commit it to the care of another? No; he layeth it on his shoulder. He placeth it near his heart. He encompasseth it with his everlasting arm, rejoicing.

He calls upon the angels to unite with him in his triumph, "Rejoice with me, for I have found my sheep which was lost."

Consider the sheep in their *state of grace.* Redeeming love has commenced the happy work. Renewing and sustaining grace carries on and completes it. Beginning with the former, the soul instantly goes on with the latter. Redeeming love, if we may so speak, is a hand stretched out to us in our direst jeopardy, pulling us out of the bottomless pit, when we were sinking, hopelessly sinking, into perdition; and taking away our foul garments from us, clothes us in the righteousness of Christ, a robe of spotless purity. Renewing grace is ready at hand to welcome us on our escape, and sets us in a chariot which bears us all along the way of holiness, straight up to the celestial gates. Redeeming love justifies us freely, instantly, and perfectly. Renewing grace sanctifies us gradually, and in the end perfectly, body, soul, and spirit.

Mark the goodness of the Divine Shepherd to his people in this state of progressive sanctification.

1. He feeds them. He provides "good pasture for them." "He leads them beside the still waters." We appeal to your own experience. When you resorted to the deceitful pastures of this world, did

they satisfy you? Did you find in its business or its pleasures that which could fill an immortal mind? No; that were impossible. But, in true religion, in vital godliness, you have found that which is solid and permanent and satisfying. You can say with truth, "He feeds me;" in the means of grace; in the dispensations of his providence; by his word, his presence. He feeds his flock like a shepherd, with food convenient for them.

2. He gives them repose. This is no less necessary than food. Hence we read: "He maketh them to lie down in green pastures." "I will feed my flock, and I will cause them to lie down, saith the Lord God." There is a striking question in Job xxxiv. 29: "When he giveth quietness, who then can make trouble?" When God smiles as a Father, who can make the child of God tremble? Can the law? The law is satisfied. Can earthly calamities? No. "God is our refuge and strength, a very present help in trouble." It was a strong thing to say (but he* who said it is now walking in white, in glory) that, "Were it possible to plunge an individual, with the peace of God in his conscience, into the depths of hell, it would be no hell to him; he might witness the torments of others,

* Rev. W. Howells, Long Acre Chapel.

but the peace of God in his conscience would shield him." "When he giveth quietness, who then can make trouble?" "The peace which passeth all understanding," which Christ bestows upon his tried and afflicted people, must be tasted to be enjoyed—must be realized experimentally, to be in the slightest degree known and appreciated.

3. He restores them. Though regenerate, they are not perfect. The old man still wars within; the evil nature still struggles for the mastery. Though they have been taught the lesson again and again, that Jesus is the supreme good for their souls, yet, through the deceitfulness of sin, they are prone to wander into forbidden paths, and to hew out to themselves cisterns of earthly comfort, broken cisterns, which can hold no water. But the Shepherd's eye is upon them; he permits them to wander a little way that they may suffer the effects of their folly; and then, he goes after them to restore and to bring them back. He heals their backslidings, because he has loved them freely. For a small moment he hides his face, that with everlasting mercies he may gather them. If he chasten them, it is but in measure, "not willingly," that he may make them "partakers of his holiness." All his dispensations have this glorious end in view.

God is determined to make his redeemed family holy in his holiness, and happy in his happiness. He visits them with one trial after another, till they are thoroughly weaned from every earthly thing; till they become as little children, distrusting themselves wholly, and trusting him wholly, for everything.

4. He protects them. They are not only weak in themselves, but absolute feebleness and helplessness. The sheep is a defenceless animal; but not so defenceless as poor, fallen man. How rich the consolation laid up for the true people of God! "He shall feed his flock like a shepherd: he shall gather the lambs with his arm, and carry them in his bosom, and shall gently lead those that are with young." They know in whom they have believed, and they are persuaded that He is able to keep that which they have committed unto him against the great day. They look into the Scriptures, and there they read the most encouraging promises. "My sheep shall never perish, neither shall any one pluck them out of my hand." Blessed be God, they have been redeemed from the hand of the enemy; they have been rescued from the fangs of the destroyer; they have been plucked as brands from the burning; and now that Christ has brought them into his fold, shall any one pluck them out of his hand, or tear

them from his heart? Impossible. Whom he loves, he loves unto the end. His grace shall be sufficient for them. He shall bruise Satan under their feet; and, finally, make them "more than conquerors" over all their spiritual foes.

5. He guides them. The shepherds in the East go before their flocks, and lead them by the voice. "The business of the day being over, we" (the missionaries of the Church of Scotland to Jerusalem, in 1839) "enjoyed a walk outside the Zion Gate. Two flocks were moving slowly up the slope of the hill, the one of goats, the other of sheep. The shepherd was going before the flock, and they followed, as he led the way toward the Jaffa Gate. We could not but remember the Saviour's words, 'When he putteth forth his own sheep, he goeth before them, and the sheep follow him, for they know his voice.' A traveller once asserted to a Syrian shepherd, that the sheep knew the *dress* of their master, not his *voice*. The shepherd, on the other hand, asserted it was the *voice* they knew. To settle the point, he and the traveller changed dresses, and went among the sheep. The traveller, in the shepherd's dress, called on the sheep, and tried to lead them; but 'they knew not his voice,' and never moved. On the other hand, they ran at

once at the call of their owner, though thus disguised."* So it is with the good Shepherd. He is the forerunner. He has gone before them, and he bids them to tread in his steps. He has left them his example, and he has promised them his strength to enable them to follow it. He guides them by his voice: they discern that voice in the Scriptures, and in the dispensations of Providence. "They follow the Lamb whithersoever he goeth:" it is the desire of their souls, "Speak, Lord, for thy servants hear."

6. How tenderly he accommodates himself to their age and weakness! He carries the lambs in his bosom, and he gently leads those that are with young. He does not "break the bruised reed, nor quench the smoking flax." He "stayeth his rough wind in the day of his east wind." He tempers the breeze to the shorn lamb. He lays affliction upon his people; but with affliction, he bestows sustaining grace. He gently leads his burdened pilgrims in his own mysterious paths; dealing with them in such matchless wisdom, and such gracious tenderness, that they are ready, with the apostle, to glory in their infirmities, that the power of Christ may rest upon them.

* Narrative of a Mission to the Jews, vol. i. p. 231.

The portion of the believer, even though his bark be tossed upon the waves of this troublesome world, is unspeakably blessed. His bitter tears shed before the cross, have real sweetness in them. And if the bitters of religion be so sweet, what are its joys? If its tears be so full of happiness, what must be comprised in its smiles?

> "If such the sweetness of the stream,
> What must the fountain be?"

God, in all his fulness; Messiah, in all his glories; the Holy Ghost, with all his shining train of satisfying and sanctifying and enlivening and ennobling influences:

> " ——— a land of pure delight,
> Where saints immortal reign;
> Infinite day excludes the night,
> And pleasures banish pain."

Bright indeed is this prospect. Glorious beyond conception are the mansions prepared for those who love and fear God. It may be asked, Is there not the valley of the shadow of death? Does not Jordan roll its dark waters between the wilderness and the heavenly Canaan? Yes. It is a solemn thing to plunge into eternity—an unaltering and unalterable eternity; for an alarming alternative presents itself: happiness or misery, life or death, heaven or hell, for ever.

If you are a partaker of the Spirit of Christ, if you desire to look to Christ alone for pardon, and to lean upon him alone for grace; if you are his sheep, brought into his fold; if you follow your Shepherd's voice, and hasten to obey his will, then death will be to you a conquered foe—we might almost say, a smiling friend. Shall that gracious God who has chosen thee, redeemed thee, regenerated thee, fed thee, restored thee, protected thee, guided thee, dealt with thee hitherto so lovingly—forsake thee, and leave thee to thyself in thy last, thy worst struggle? No. The valley of the shadow of death may be dark, but it is safe and short; for God, thy God, will be with thee, his rod and his staff they shall comfort thee. Some of us have been privileged to witness how the Lord can sustain his people in their dying moments. We know too, in olden days, how he endued the noble army of martyrs with zeal and courage, to meet death in its most terrific aspect. When Bishop Hooper was martyred, though his sufferings were wantonly protracted for three-quarters of an hour; though three times the fire was made up, green fagots having been ordered to try the strength of his patience and endurance, as it were, to the uttermost—yet this is the testimony of the historian to his faith: "Thus was he three-quarters of an hour in the fire. Even as a lamb (one from Christ's fold), he patiently bore the extremity thereof, neither moving backwards nor forwards, nor to any side, but died as quietly as a child in his bed."

Patrick Hamilton was the first preacher and martyr of the Scottish Reformation. He suffered for Christ in 1528. Six hours was he in burning. "At noon," says his biographer,* "he was seated at a table in an apartment of the castle, awaiting calmly the signal for setting out to the closing scene. The martyr was ready for the stake, and the stake for the martyr. The spirit of power and of love had fallen abundantly upon him, and the most perfect composure, resolution, and self-devotion filled his soul. When the hour of noon struck, he sent for the captain, and inquired whether all was ready. The captain, more humane than his master, was unable to tell him plainly the fatal truth; he could only hint that the last hour was even come. Hamilton immediately rose from his seat, and putting his hand into the captain's walked forth with a quick step towards the place of execution. He carried in

* Abridged from Lorimer's Life of Patrick Hamilton.

his right hand a copy of the evangelists, and was accompanied by his servant, and a few intimate friends. When he came in sight of the spot, he uncovered his head, and addressed himself in silent prayer to Him who alone could give him a martyr's strength and victory. On reaching the stake, he handed to one of his friends the precious volume which had long been his companion, and the 'rod of his strength;' and taking off his cap and gown, and other upper garments, he gave them to his attendant, with the words, 'These will not profit in the fire: they will profit thee. After this, of me thou canst receive no commodity, except the example of my death, which I pray thee bear in mind. For albeit it be bitter to the flesh, and fearful before man, yet is it the entrance to eternal life, which none shall possess that denies Christ Jesus before this wicked generation.' After an ineffectual effort to make him recant, he was fastened to the stake by an iron chain round his middle. Fire was now laid to the pile, and exploded some powder which was placed among the fagots. The martyr's left hand and left cheek were scorched by the explosion; but though thrice kindled, the flames took no steady hold of the pile. 'Have you no dry wood?' demanded the sufferer. 'Have you no more gunpowder?' It was some time before fresh billets and powder could be fetched from the castle, and his sufferings during the interval were extremely acute.

"After a while the flames were rekindled; a baker, called Myrton, brought his arms full of straw and cast it into the fire; whereupon there came a blast of wind from the east, and raised the flame of fire so vehemently that it blew upon the friar who had accused him, and threw him upon the ground, burning all the fore-part of his cowl. The terror and confusion of the conscience-stricken Dominican contrasted strangely with the calmness of the martyr. Surrounded and devoured by fierce flames, he had still recollectedness enough to remember, in his torment, his widowed mother, and to commend her with his dying breath to the care and sympathy of his friends. When nearly burnt through his middle by the fiery chain, a voice in the crowd of spectators called aloud to him, that if he still had faith in the doctrine for which he died, he should give a last sign of his constancy. Whereupon he raised three fingers of his half-consumed hand, and held them steadily in that position till he ceased to live. His last audible words were, 'How long, Lord, shall darkness overwhelm this kingdom? How long wilt thou suffer this tyranny of man? Lord Jesus, receive my spirit.'

"The execution had lasted for nearly six hours; 'but during all that time,' says Alexander Alane, who had witnessed with profound emotion the whole scene, 'the martyr never gave one sign of impatience or anger, nor ever called to heaven for vengeance upon his persecutors: so great was his faith; so strong his confidence in God.'"

Thus tragically but gloriously died, on the 29th of February, 1528, Patrick Hamilton—a noble martyr in a noble cause.

These instances, while they clearly evince what Popery is when in power, how cruel and how intolerant; also illustrate in the most striking manner the vital power of Christianity to give consolation and support under the most terrible sufferings.

If the dealings of Christ, the good Shepherd, are so gracious towards his people in the chequered path of life, and in the hour of dissolution, how can we describe the glory which he has prepared for them in the world to come? "It doth not yet appear what we shall be: but we know that, when he shall appear, we shall be like him; for we shall see him as he is." "Eye hath not seen, nor ear heard, neither have entered into the heart of man, the things which God hath prepared for them that love him." They "have washed their robes, and made them white in the blood of the Lamb. Therefore are they before the throne of God, and serve him day and night in his temple: and he that sitteth on the throne shall dwell among them. They shall hunger no more; neither thirst any more, neither shall the sun light on them, nor any heat. For the Lamb which is in the midst of the throne shall feed them, and shall lead them unto living fountains of waters: and God shall wipe away all tears from their eyes."

How may we know whether we are Christ's sheep? His sheep are marked in the *ear* and in the *foot.* "My sheep *hear* my voice, and they *follow* me." The Lord grant that we may have, manifestly and unquestionably, the *mark* of his chosen flock, his faithful people.

"THE RESURRECTION AND THE LIFE."

"Jesus said unto her, I am the resurrection, and the life: he that believeth in me, though he were dead, yet shall he live: and whosoever liveth and believeth in me shall never die. Believest thou this?"—JOHN xi. 25, 26.

THIS is the address of Jesus to Martha, when she had, in conformity with the general opinion of the Jews, expressed her belief in the resurrection at the last day. "Jesus saith unto her, Thy brother shall rise again. Martha saith unto him, I know that he shall rise again in the resurrection at the last day." She plainly inferred, "What comfort can this minister to me now?" Observe the weakness of Martha's faith. She could believe the distant miracle, when the ten thousand times ten thousand inhabitants of this earth shall rise at the last day; but she could not realize the present assurance, that that brother, whom she so fondly loved, should, even then, at the word of Jesus, arise from his sepulchre at Bethany. It is the triumph of faith to receive humbly, to rest cheerfully upon the promise for *to-day;* amidst daily wants, trials, and temptations, to believe that "as our days, so shall our strength be;" and that as each season of difficulty occurs, there will accompany it, grace, and love, and patience, equal to our need and God's requirement.

"Jesus said unto her, I am the resurrection." What comfort must these words have brought to Martha and Mary! "By my own power, shall the resurrection take place; if I can raise up the countless myriads of mankind who have been dead so many ages, cannot I raise up one man who has been dead four days? What then have you to fear, either for Lazarus or for yourselves? I tell you that he shall rise again, and I can command the resurrection which I promise." Here was power more astonishing than the imagination could conceive, united to mercy more tender than the heart could venture to hope.

"I am the resurrection." What a proof does this title afford of the Divine glory of Jesus, for who but God can raise the dead? Yet Jesus here claims this as his own: "I am the resurrection." "I have the keys of hell and of death." "Marvel not at this: for the hour is coming, in the which all that are in the graves shall hear his voice, and shall come forth: they that have done good, unto the resurrection of life; and they that have done evil, unto the resurrection of damnation." In the day of his humiliation, he raised three persons from the grave: an only daughter, an only son, and, in the case under consideration, an only brother. This he did in his own name, and by his own power. "Talitha cumi." "Young man, I say unto thee, Arise." "Lazarus, come forth."

A further illustration of this glorious title was afforded in Christ's own resurrection. To each person of the sacred Trinity is this mighty work ascribed. That he was raised by the Father's power, we read in Acts ii. 32, "This Jesus hath God raised up;" and in Eph. i. 20, "Which He (that is, the Father) wrought in Christ, when he raised him from the dead, and set him at his own right hand in the heavenly places." That he was raised by the power of the Spirit, we read in Rom. viii. 11, "If the Spirit of him that raised up Jesus from the dead dwell in you;" and in 1 Pet. iii. 18, "Put to death in the flesh, but quickened by the Spirit." And that Christ raised himself up, we read in John x. 18, "No man taketh it from me, but I lay it down of myself. I have power to lay it down, and I have power to take it again;" and ii. 19, "Destroy this temple, and in three days I will raise it up.—He spoke of the temple of his body." Christ's resurrection is the corner-stone of our spiritual hopes: "If Christ be not raised, your faith is vain; ye are yet in your sins." He "bare our sins in his own body on the tree." "He tasted death for every man." He "was made a curse for us," as our gracious Substitute and Surety. "The whole cup (says Bishop Hopkins) of that fury and wrath of God which we should have been drinking off, drop by drop, throughout eternity, Christ drank off at once." The full penalty of the law, he paid. Had he remained in the grave, where would have been the proof that his payment for us had been accepted by the Father? So long as the law has a just hold upon a man, so long does he remain in prison. If Christ had remained in the prison of the grave, it might have been argued that his work was not sufficient, and that his satisfaction to the justice of God was not complete. But as he died for our sins, so he rose for our justification. He was buried, to show the reality of his death; he rested in the grave till the third day, that the prophetic word might be fulfilled. An angel was sent to remove the stone from the mouth of the sepulchre: "The Father, to testify that his justice was fully satisfied with the price which the Son had paid, sent an officer from heaven to open the doors of the grave, and, as it were, to hold away the hangings while his Lord came forth from his bed-chamber." * How truly happy must those be who are interested in the death and resurrection of Jesus! "Who shall lay anything to the charge of God's elect? It is God that justifieth. Who is he that condemneth? It is Christ that died, yea rather, that is risen again, who is even at the right hand of God, who also maketh intercession for us."

Another illustration of this title occurs every day. "I am the resurrection," saith the Lord Jesus. What are we in our natural state? "Dead in trespasses and sins." What is Christ's command to us? "Awake thou that sleepest, and arise from the dead, and Christ shall give thee light." What is the fact when the soul is quickened with Divine energy?—"made willing in the day of God's power." "This my son," saith the Lord, "was dead, and is alive again." This is the work of Christ. He is the fountain of life and light. In every case of real conversion of heart, he says to us, "I am the resurrection."

* Bishop Reynolds.

We shall witness a grand display of the truth of this title when the resurrection morn shall dawn upon this earth. What multitudes shall then awake, some to everlasting life, some to shame and everlasting contempt! Christ's resurrection is a pledge of our resurrection. "Every man in his own order: Christ the first-fruits; afterward they that are Christ's at his coming." "Because he lives, we shall live also." "In a moment, in the twinkling of an eye, at the last trump: for the trumpet shall sound, and the dead shall be raised incorruptible, and we shall be changed. For this corruptible must put on incorruption, and this mortal must put on immortality. So when this corruptible shall have put on incorruption, and this mortal shall have put on immortality, then shall be brought to pass the saying that is written, Death is swallowed up in victory. O death, where is thy sting? O grave, where is thy victory?"

"I am the resurrection, and the life." Life is no less necessary than resurrection. The life which Jesus imparts to his people must be sustained by him. What the vine is to the branches, and the head to the members, Jesus is to his believing people. The life which they live in the flesh, they live by faith of the Son of God, who hath loved them, and hath given himself for them; and "when Christ, who is their life, shall appear, then shall they also appear with him in glory." This we shall enter into more fully, if we consider the promise that follows: "He that believeth in me, though he were dead, yet shall he live."

"Though he were dead." Whatever may have been the sinner's previous state of rebellion; however great his transgressions; "though he were dead," yet by faith, wrought in his heart by the Holy Spirit, "he shall live:" the first acting of faith is the first acting of spiritual life, the earnest of everlasting life. The penitent may be tempted to regard his case as almost desperate. His sins may seem steep and rugged as mountains, boisterous as the waves of the sea, more numerous than the hairs of the head. But in this promise there is rich encouragement: "He that believeth, *though he were dead*, yet shall he live." Come, O trembling sinner, to Jesus, just as thou art. Accept him as thy Saviour. Welcome him to the throne of thy heart; and thou "shalt live."

"Though he were dead." How frequently is the believer constrained to make the mournful confession of the psalmist, "My soul cleaveth unto the dust," and to offer his prayer, "Quicken thou me according to thy word." Art thou ready to faint,

O believer, with thy long and weary conflict? Art thou cast down at the remembrance of thy many acts of ingratitude and unfaithfulness to thy Lord? Does it appear to thee, as if day by day thy way were more steep, thy temptations more urgent, and thy realization of eternal things more slender? Has the world laid its withering hand upon thee, and hast thou been so torn by solicitations from outward things, on the right and on the left, that thou hast suffered an estrangement to spring up between thy soul and Jesus? Is the Bible a sealed book to thee? Hast thou no boldness of access to the mercy seat? Are the ordinances of religion wearisome formalities? Dost thou appear to thyself as if thou wert now "twice dead?" Does the enemy suggest that there is no hope? Nay, does he even quote Scripture to remind thee that it is "impossible to renew thee to repentance?" Oh listen to the gracious promise, "He that believeth, though he were dead," yet, on the renewal of faith, there shall be the renewal of life. Believe on Him who is "the resurrection and the life." Only acknowledge thine iniquity; keep nothing back; conceal nothing; palliate nothing; say, "Lord, here is a poor, dead soul: I plead thy promise;" "I believe, help thou mine unbelief;" though I am dead, make me to live. How graciously will he receive, and how tenderly will he embrace, and how freely will he forgive such a returning, believing soul!

"Though he were dead." The bodies of the saints must undergo the sentence of death pronounced against sin. "The body is dead because of sin." Their souls shall never die, and their bodies shall be reanimated, and made like unto their Redeemer's glorious body. The doctrine of the resurrection of the body may appear impossible to human reason, and it was opposed by the ancient heathen on this very ground. When a Christian was slain for his profession of faith in Jesus, they burned his body, and cast the ashes into the river, that they might be carried into the broad ocean, and be made the sport of winds and waves. And by this they thought to prove the impossibility of a resurrection. Bishop Hopkins well answers this argument; for he remarks that "unless the parts of the body could be scattered beyond the reach of Almighty power; unless they could be crumbled into so small a size as to escape the knowledge and care of God, who arranges every little particle of dust that plays up and down in the sunbeam; then the scattering of the parts of the body far and wide does not prove the impossibility of their being united again: for the power and providence of God will gather up every atom of their dust, and rally them together into there present order and place."

There is, however, no occasion to defend this doctrine by an appeal to the omnipotence and omniscience of the Deity. Professor Hitchcock* has ably shown, in his lecture on the "Resurrections of Spring," that the doctrine of the resurrection of the body is taught in the Bible; that the germ of the resurrection body proceeds from the body that is laid in the grave; that our present organization does not exist in the resurrection body; "that flesh and blood cannot inherit the kingdom of God;" that there will be as great a difference between our present bodies and the spiritual body, as between the seed and the full-grown plant that proceeds from it. "That which thou sowest, thou sowest not that body that shall be, but bare grain, it may chance of wheat, or of some other grain; but God giveth it a body as it hath pleased him." "Consider," observes this author, "how few particles of the seed enter into the composition of the plant that springs from it. Compare, for instance, a forest tree weighing many tons, with the seed weighing a few grains, from which it sprang; and then, recollect also, that

* "Peculiar Phenomena of the Four Seasons."

only a small part of the seed finds its way into the future plant; and we may safely say that the proportion between the particles derived from the seed and from other sources, is only as one to a million. Yet the Bible justifies the conclusion, that equally small may be the proportion of the particles derived from our present bodies in the resurrection body. If only a millionth part, or a ten thousandth millionth part of the matter deposited in the grave, shall be raised from thence, it justifies the representations of Scripture, that there will be a resurrection of the dead. And why may we not suppose, that amid the transmutations which the dead body may undergo, some infinitesimal germ may be watched over by Omniscience, and by Omnipotence at length be made to constitute the germ of the spiritual body? This body will possess a specific and individual identity. 'God giveth' to the plant that springs from the wheat, or other seed sown, 'a body as it hath pleased him, and to every seed his own body;' that is, a peculiar body, one marked off from every other. The apostle illustrates this statement, as if it were a point of great importance. 'All flesh,' says he, 'is not the same flesh; but there is one kind of flesh of men, another flesh of beasts, another of fishes, and another of birds.'

He states the same fact respecting organic bodies: 'There are also celestial bodies, and bodies terrestrial: but the glory of the celestial is one, and the glory of the terrestrial is another. There is one glory of the sun, and another glory of the moon, and another glory of the stars; for one star differeth from another star in glory. So also,' he adds, 'is the resurrection of the dead.' And he teaches that there will be a peculiarity of character that will discriminate between the resurrection body and everything else; and he implies that even individual peculiarities will exist in a future world."

In our present state we can form no idea of the spiritual body. Three particulars are mentioned by the apostle: "It is sown in corruption, it is raised in incorruption; it is sown in dishonour, it is raised in glory; it is sown in weakness, it is raised in power." This statement, so far as we can realize it, gives us a very exalted conception of the nature and glory of the resurrection body. The same writer has shown that "there is no necessity for an identity of particles to establish the identity of the spiritual and natural body." "What is it," he asks, "that constitutes bodily identity in this world? Suppose a person born in this country (America), after living here twenty years, goes to China for a permanent residence. Now, as we have reason to suppose that the entire particles of which a man is composed change every seven years, this individual, after residing ten years in China, will not probably retain in his composition a single particle of the body which he acquired in America. But he is still the same man, and why? Because his body is made up of the same kinds of elementary matter combined in the same proportion as in America, and has the same form and structure. And it matters not whence the elements of a compound are derived, whether from China or the United States; if they are only united in the same proportion, they will constitute exactly the same substance. Thus, it can make no difference from what source the oxygen and hydrogen are obtained, that form water. It will be identically the same substance, though its elements come from the antipodes. So it is with the oxygen, hydrogen, carbon, nitrogen, phosphorus, and lime that make up the human system. The essential thing that makes them the flesh and bones of man, is their combination in a certain definite proportion. And though there may be a constant loss of individual particles, yet if their place is supplied with others of the same kind, no matter whence they come, they will maintain the identity of the body, if combined in the proper proportion; for it is essentially the chemical composition, not the identity of particles, that continues a man the same from year to year. If this be a correct view of what constitutes personal identity in this world, we have only to apply it to the resurrection body in order to meet satisfactorily the famous objection to the resurrection of the body, that its particles enter into the composition of several other bodies. By this view, *it is not necessary that the resurrection body should contain a single particle of the body laid in the grave;* if it only contain particles of the same kind, united in the same proportion, and the compound be made to assume the same form and structure as the natural body. For all this is what often happens to men in this world, without exciting a suspicion that the identity of the individual is endangered. God may give to the man raised from the grave such a body as pleases him, just as he does to the plant; but if it be only composed of the same elements in the same proportion, and have a peculiarity of form and structure, its identity with the individual buried will be preserved."

Our limits will allow us to abridge but one more extract from the valuable lecture to which we have been so largely indebted. Having deduced several interesting analogies from the "Season of Spring," Professor Hitchcock observes, that "spring restores to us many well-remembered forms of vegetable and animal life. When the frosts of autumn came on, it was saddening to see many familiar forms of the vegetable world, to which we had become attached, yielding up their foliage; and though they descended to the grave in a gaudy dress, we could not but feel that we were losing the society of friends. Then, too, the song of the birds ceased in the fields and the woods, or they uttered only a few solitary and farewell notes, as they withdrew to their southern retreats. Yet with the opening spring they have come back: in a new dress indeed, but still the same, and awakening delightful reminiscences and anticipations. Some of them have been concealed among us, and subjected to the stern power of winter: and others have fled far away to escape his withering blasts. But they have reappeared, as fresh and lovely as ever; yea, more so: nor can we perceive that one feature is gone, or changed, save that the fresher charms of youth are upon them.

"How delightful to be able to say, Thus shall it be with the resurrection of the dead! Then shall the grave deliver up a multitude of well-remembered and endeared forms, which in sadness we committed to its charge. What consolation does this offer to the bereaved! Who has not been afflicted by the removal of those whose forms and features have been ever since remembered with the deepest interest? We have called in the aid, it may be, of painting and photography, to embalm their features, and the expression which the workings of the soul within gave to the countenance. And how deep was our anguish, when we last looked upon them, as we saw the grave closing over their remains! But if they were the true disciples of Christ, they shall be restored to us in the resurrection morning; and we shall recognize them amid the millions who then awake from the grave, as we now recognize the plants and birds of spring. There shall be a characteristic something in their spiritual bodies, that will lead us at once, and with exulting joy, to fly to their embrace. Oh, blessed season of recognition and joy! How will it wipe away every Christian's tears, and restore him to his departed friends, and bring them all together in the presence of their Lord, to enjoy his smiles and the delightful intercourse of one another, with no fear of change or separation, for ever and ever! Oh that this bright hope might stimulate us so to live and to labour, that not only we ourselves, but all whom we love on earth shall come forth at the resurrection of the just, purified from the stains and sins of earth, and ripe for the perfect holiness and happiness of heaven!"

If the reunion of saints, and their recognition of each other on the resurrection morning, be so richly fraught with an ever-increasing happiness and glory, what shall we think of the meeting of sinners with sinners before the Judge at the great day? Mr. Moffat in one of his journeys fell in with an African king surrounded by his court: he was employed in making arrows and spears. Mr. Moffat began talking to him; and he told him of the resurrection, which he described in vivid colours. And as he went on, he saw that the iron man's face began to work convulsively; the muscles began to quiver; the eyes were looking as though they would start from his head; and when he was able to speak—for he trembled all over—he said, "What! what do you say? Shall I see all the men I have slaughtered on the field of battle? Do you mean to say that they will all rise up before me, and that I shall know them, and that they will know me? Do you mean to say that I shall see them there, with all their wounds, just as I slew them?" He dreaded the sight of the victims of his valour, as he once thought, but of his cruelty, as he now began to think. Yes, that man will know all his victims. Companions in crime here will be companions in misery there. Every sinner has his victims here. Every sinner shall meet and recognize his victims there. Before the great white throne, in the presence of an assembled universe, and amidst the blaze of an opening eternity, sinners shall recognize those whom they have seduced and destroyed in this world. It is related of the historian Hume, that he destroyed the faith of his poor mother by giving her arguments against Christianity. On the bed of death she found those arguments could not support her; she sent for her son to tell him that she was sinking into eternity with nothing under her feet. Hume shall meet his mother; and the mother shall meet the son who did this awful work. Let us "not be deceived; God is not mocked: for whatsoever a man soweth, that shall he also reap. For he that soweth to the flesh shall of the flesh reap corruption; but he that soweth to the Spirit shall of the Spirit reap life everlasting."

We have tarried so long on this interesting topic that we have left ourselves no space for the consideration of the latter clause of our Lord's promise:

"He that liveth and believeth in me shall never die."

"He that *liveth* and believeth." Life is the seed-time for eternity. It is the only season for conversion to God. How important, then, and how valuable is life! "He that liveth," and by grace "believeth" in Jesus, "shall never die;" for the "gift of God is eternal life through Jesus Christ our Lord."

This promise has also a spiritual reference: "He that liveth and believeth;" he that evinces his spiritual life by his faith in the Son of God, and by the fruits of faith in his walk and conversation, "shall never die," but shall pass through the portal of death to everlasting glory.

Reader, let me press this grave inquiry upon your attention. "Believest thou this," that Jesus is the "resurrection and the life?" Canst thou realize the solemnities of the great day? Where will be thy place? On the right hand, or on the left hand of the Judge? With what emotions wilt thou recognize thy companions here? What is the character of the seed which thou art sowing? Will thy harvest be everlasting joy, or "shame and everlasting contempt?" What reply does conscience make to these inquiries?—"Jesus saith, I am the resurrection and the life; believest thou this?" Canst thou say with Martha, "Yea, Lord?" If so, then, in adoring gratitude, ascribe the faith which has been wrought in thy heart, with its present peace and glorious anticipations, to the grace of God; and "let your light so shine before men, that they may see your good works, and glorify your Father which is in heaven."

"MASTER AND LORD."

"Ye call me Master, and Lord: and ye say well; for so I am."
—JOHN xiii. 13.

SOLEMN indeed was the occasion when these words were spoken. "Jesus knew that his hour was come, that he should depart out of this world unto the Father;" the hour predetermined in the counsels of eternity, to which he had eagerly looked forward, when by his sacrifice upon the cross he should achieve redemption for man, and vindicate all the attributes of God. This hour now had almost arrived, and the moments that intervened he occupied in comforting and instructing his disciples. Surely, next to the hour of the crucifixion, the time spent with his disciples in the upper chamber in Jerusalem was the most solemn in the history of man. The condescension and grace with which the Lord of all became the servant of all when he washed the disciples' feet, suggest many reflections to the thoughtful Christian. For not only did he teach impressively the important lessons of humility and love to the brethren, but he also illustrated by this significant action the object for which he came into the world, and the amazing sacrifices required of him in its accomplishment. We must not, however, pause to meditate upon the sublime mysteries wrapped up in this narrative, but proceed to the consideration of the titles which our Lord assumed, when, having again taken his seat at the table, he said, "Know ye what I have done to you? Ye call me Master, and Lord: and ye say well; for so I am. If I then, your Lord and Master, have washed your feet, ye also ought to wash one another's feet."

By the title of "Lord" is implied the Divine glory of Jesus. It was his Deity which added such a halo to his condescension, and such solemnity to the lessons of humility which he drew from it. As we have in previous chapters adduced many illustrations and proofs of this important and consolatory doctrine, we will not return to it, but direct our attention to the dominion which Christ exercises over his people. There is an important passage on this subject in Rom. xiv. 7–9. The apostle has been urging upon the Christians at Rome, the duty of liberality to the opinions of others in minor points. And he reminds them that "none of us liveth to himself, and no man dieth to himself. For whether we live, we live unto the Lord; and whether we die, we die unto the Lord: whether we live therefore, or die, we are the Lord's. For to this end Christ both died, and rose, and revived, that he might be Lord both of the dead and living." Scott remarks on these verses that "no real Christian allows his own humour, indulgence, interest, credit, or ease, to be the end for which he lives or acts, as to the general tenor of his conduct; nor does he even avoid, desire, or meet death from selfish motives: but whether his life be prolonged, he aims to spend it to the glory of Christ; or whether death be expected, he refers it to him, to be ordered in all respects for the glory of his name. So that whether the Christian lives or dies, he belongs to the Lord to be disposed of as he pleases; and as the object of his love, to be taken care of by him in all possible events. For to this very end Christ both died on the cross, and rose again, and liveth in heaven to die no more; that in human nature he might be the sovereign Lord of all his people, both during their lives and after their death, as they willingly devote themselves to him, and are prompt to labour, suffer, or die for his sake; as he orders all things respecting the time and circumstances of their death, for his own glory and their good; and as, when they die, they are taken to be with him for ever, and he will raise their bodies to share the same felicity."

As our Creator, the Lord Jesus has a claim upon all we have and all we are. He hath made us, and not we ourselves; or as it is in the margin, "His we are," Psa. c. 3. We are his workmanship; he fashioned us in the womb; he has covered us with skin and flesh; fenced us with bones and sinews; he has poured into our nostrils the breath of life, and the inspiration of the Almighty has given us understanding. Suppose we were to return to him all that we received from him, what would be left of our own? His right, then, to us as our Creator is complete. He has a property in us, not only such as no man can have in a fallen creature, but such as even no father has in his own children. They are his in a subordinate and limited degree; but we are the Lord's absolutely and entirely.

As the providential disposer of our lot, Christ has a claim to all our love and obedience. "By him all things consist," and "in him we live, and move, and have our being." Are we not indebted to him for the countless blessings and comforts which we enjoy? Has not he made this world beautiful, even in its ruins? Has not he, by the medium of the atmosphere, tempered light to our powers of vision? Has not he made green, so sweet and soothing a colour to the eye, the prevailing colour of the landscape? Has not he so constituted the atmosphere in such admirable proportions, that we can inspire and respire it, not only without difficulty, but without consciousness? Has not he watched over us individually, with tender care? Has not he sustained us amidst the perils of infancy? Has not he renewed his mercies every morning? Has not he given his beloved sleep? Has not he, in wisdom, appointed the bounds of our habitation, and in love upheld and guided us from day to day? Has not he "made all things work together for our good," taught us, in the way of discipline, how to obtain "honey from the rock, and meat from the eater?" Has not he healed many sorrows, wiped away many tears, answered many prayers, and opened before us, by means as suitable as unexpected, a path in the wilderness and streams in the desert? What shall we say to these blessings? Should they not constrain us to yield ourselves to him? Shall we not be most vile if we do not acknowledge our untold obligations?

Christ is our Lord, as our Redeemer. "We are not our own," for we have been "bought with a price," not "with corruptible things, as silver and gold, but with the precious blood of Christ, as of a lamb without blemish and without spot." The magnificence of creation arose at the simple fiat of Christ. "By the word of the Lord were the heavens made; and all the host of them by the breath of his mouth." To make a watch requires skill. But when that watch has been dashed upon the stones, and broken into ten thousand pieces, then to gather up the fragments, and arrange them, and reconstruct the watch, would be a work of acknowledged difficulty, and of surpassing skill. Creation was a great work; but redemption was infinitely greater. Israel was redeemed out of Egypt by the power of God, "with a mighty hand and a stretched-out arm." But the Exodus involved no incarnation, no sacrifice. How vast the cost at which our redemption has been procured! God himself must assume our nature, and in that nature obey the law's utmost demand, and suffer its severest penalty. Let us meditate upon the spotless life of Christ, and his agonizing death, that we may realize his claim to the allegiance of our hearts.

> "Were the whole realm of nature mine,
> That were a present far too small:
> Love so amazing, so Divine,
> Demands my soul, my life, my all."

To inflame our gratitude, let us reflect upon the depth of sin and misery from which he has rescued us. He has "brought us up out of an horrible pit, out of the miry clay," from the power of darkness, from this present evil world, from the wrath of God, and from the flames of hell.

Let us survey the blessedness of salvation to which Christ has raised us. "He has set our feet upon the rock, and established our goings. He has put a new song into our mouth, even praise unto our God." He has adopted us into his family, and has enabled us to cry, "Abba, Father." He has given us, even here, a joy that is unspeakable, and a "peace that passeth all understanding;" and he has dignified us by making us the channels of his mercy to others, and the happy instruments of glorifying his name.

All these mercies have been bestowed upon us in a way adapted to our circumstances as sinners. He has appointed faith as the medium of union and communion with himself. Faith is a grace which requires nothing from us but the acknowledgment of our emptiness, and poverty, and unworthiness, and which pleads with God his own sure promise and unchanging love. Faith is not the natural fruit of the heart, but the gift of God, through the operation of the Holy Spirit. And, blessed be God, he has freely promised the Holy Spirit to all who ask him in humble prayer for this inestimable benefit. The redemption of Christ is all of grace. The more we examine its provisions, the more sensible shall we be of the claim of Jesus to our devoted service and unwavering confidence.

If we are his loving disciples, we have ratified the claim of Jesus to be Lord of our hearts. We have surrendered ourselves to him. We have "joined ourselves to the Lord by a perpetual covenant, that shall never be forgotten." "We have subscribed with our hand unto the Lord, and surnamed ourselves by the name of Israel." We can look back with shame upon the time when other lords—the world, the flesh, and the devil—had dominion over us. Perhaps we can remember the occasion which, by grace, led us to make the wise and happy choice. Perhaps we were under sore trial when we first lifted up our heart to the great God; perhaps it was the conversation of a friend, or the perusal of a religious book, or the faithful preaching of the cross, that was blessed by God to subdue our hearts to the "obedience of faith." Perhaps we can recall the emotions with which we first prayed, or wrote out a prayer, and with tears of contrition signed our name to make the hallowed transaction more permanent. Can we look back upon all this, and not adore and magnify the grace which has been manifested towards us? Have we any feeling of regret for the step which we then took? Nay, has it not been our happiness again and again to renew our covenant?—in the hour of retirement — in the field of meditation — in the house of God, and at his holy table. Have we not said, Lord, I am thine; I offer and present myself to thee; my understanding shall be thine, to know thee; my will to choose thee; my conscience to fear thee; my tongue shall set forth thy praise; my life shall be devoted to thy glory?

It would not be difficult to illustrate these observations by incidents from real life. Martin Luther was one day searching in the library of the university of Erfurt, when he found a large volume, with strong clasps, covered with dust. It was the Bible: he had never seen it before. He knew nothing more of the Bible than the lessons extracted from it in the Missal, or the incidental histories given from it in the Breviary. He began to read that Bible: he found in it new and awakening facts. He read of the guilt of man so deep that no tears could wash it away, and of the holiness of God so awful that no sinner could meet it. He trembled and he read: he read again and again; he trembled, and wept, and read. The Reformation with all its issues, stretching into eternal ages, was contained in the dusty Bible Martin Luther discovered at Erfurt. God's providence seconded the teaching of his grace. Luther was one day walking in the fields with a fellow-student, when a storm of thunder and lightning overtook them; both ran for shelter, but ere they reached a place of retreat, Luther's companion was struck by the lightning, and dropped dead at Luther's feet. Luther was unscathed. That companion the world could do without, but neither the world nor the church could do without Luther. This solemn event impressed and awed the spirit of Luther. He felt with increasing force, Life how short!—Judgment how near!—Eternity how terrible! When he recollected what his own conscience felt, and what God's word declared, and thought that he also might be struck by the next flash, or overwhelmed by the next storm, and sent to stand shivering and naked and guilty at the judgment seat, he endured an agony of spirit that was beyond all expression. "What," he asked himself, "what must I do to be saved? What can I do?" He cried out in the anguish of his soul, "Oh my sin! my sin! what, what can forgive me my sin?" Such was the commencement of Luther's spiritual life.

Many have been awakened to the service of God during a storm at sea. John Newton, once a libertine and an infidel, once a dealer in slaves on the coast of Africa, and himself the slave of evil passions, was, after years of hardened rebellion against God, led, during an awful tempest, to examine his own heart, to read the New Testament, and to pray for the gift of the Holy Spirit. His life was preserved through many imminent perils, and, "being found faithful," he was admitted into the sacred ministry. For several years, at Olney, he preached the faith which once he sought to destroy. There he formed a friendship with Thomas Scott, whom he directed into the truth as it is in Jesus, and who was the author of the Commentary on the Bible of world-wide fame and usefulness.

Our glorious God, who binds the ocean with a rope of sand, and sustains millions of created things by the dew-drops of the morning, often employs very feeble means for the production of very grand results in the moral and spiritual world. What can be more insignificant than a tract? In the hand of God, nevertheless, one of these little messengers can convey light to the mind, and life to the heart, and civilization to regions lying in darkness and the shadow of death.

That well-known tract, "The Dairyman's Daughter," written in the Isle of Wight by the Rev. Legh Richmond, found its way to Constantinople. There it was translated into the Armenian tongue by the Rev. Dr. Goodell, an American missionary to Turkey. A copy of this version was carried to Nicomedia, and fell into the hands of a *vartabed* or preaching priest of the Armenian church. He, upon perusing it, was deeply affected by the picture it presented of simple and genuine Christianity, such as he supposed to have existed only amongst the primitive Christians. Comparing the spirit and principles of this sweet story with the condition of the corrupt Armenian church, he was led to the study of the New Testament, and the result was his own conversion. He then communicated the knowledge of this wondrous tract, and his own blessed experience, to another *vartabed* with the same results. These two converted priests, expelled from their own corrupt communion, were the founders of the evangelical church now existing in Nicomedia. That church has given origin to two others in the neighbourhood; and as the good influence extends itself widely in all directions, it is impossible to say how far throughout Turkey may yet be diffused the beneficial leaven of the "Dairyman's Daughter." Thus the church of Nicomedia commenced in the Isle of Wight.

Jesus Christ is not only the Lord, but also the Master of his believing people. The original word for Master signifies Teacher, and is so translated in John iii. 2. "Rabbi, we know that thou art a teacher come from God." This title of "Teacher" which he assumed, suggests some profitable hints for our meditation.

Christ is a "Teacher sent from God." If the Lord of heaven and the "Prince of the kings of the earth" condescend to teach us, with what reverence and humility does it become us to "sit at his feet and hear his word!"

As a Teacher, Christ has infinite knowledge. From eternity he was in the bosom of the Father, and knew all the counsels and purposes of God. His comprehensive eye journeys in an instant throughout the regions of space, and contemplates the innumerable worlds which he has created, with all their teeming populations; and his tender solicitude is engaged in directing the affairs of the meanest of his servants. He "knows the things that come into their mind—every one of them." If a sparrow be not forgotten by him, will he overlook one of his own disciples? No; Christ knows all things, all events and persons in heaven, on earth, and in hell. He knows the mind of God, and the circumstances of his people; and he is therefore able to guide them into all truth needful for their peace here, and for their happiness hereafter.

As a Teacher, Christ is characterized by gentleness and consideration for his pupils. He does not sew a new piece upon an old garment, nor "put new wine into old bottles." Christ teaches his disciples as they are able to bear.

He manifests great patience towards their infirmities. He teaches them the same lesson again and again—"precept upon precept; line upon line; here a little, and there a little."

Jesus Christ teaches by his example: I have given you an example, that ye should do as I have done to you. The original word for example, in 1 Pet. ii. 21, is very instructive. It denotes a copy set for children to write under and imitate without one false stroke. Christ has written out for us, in his life, the will of God. See how I teach you to obey: "come and learn of me; for I am meek and lowly in heart: and ye shall find rest unto your souls." Christ is a commander like Gideon, who said to his soldiers, "Look on me, and do likewise;" and like Cæsar, who called his soldiers, not "soldiers," but "fellow-soldiers," and whose usual word was not "Go," but "Come."

Christ teaches effectually, for he teaches by the Spirit. Ministers and parents can only inform the understanding, but they cannot sanctify the heart. Who teaches like Christ? By his Spirit he pours light into the soul, applies his word to the conscience, and draws the heart gently, yet powerfully, to faith, love, and holy obedience. Five minutes' instruction in Christ's school is worth more than ten thousand sermons.

We have seen a child make a drawing from a picture set before him; and as the work grows under his pencil, he is delighted with his own performance, and does not perceive its many defects. The master looks at the work, and surprises the pupil by pointing out deficiencies hitherto unsuspected; he then takes the pencil into his hand, and by a bold touch here, and a stroke there, he produces a new effect; so that the pupil is at once astonished and humbled. Thus a touch or so from the Spirit of Jesus in the heart, is more effectual than all the wisdom of the schools, and all the learning of the ancients. Let us inquire, Have we so learned Christ? Devout Mr. Herbert, when he mentioned the name of *Christ*, used to add, *my Master;* and thus expresses himself concerning it in one of his poems:

> "How sweetly doth 'my Master' sound! 'my Master!'
> As ambergis leaves a rich scent
> Unto the taster,
> So do these words a sweet content,
> An oriental fragrancy; 'my Master.'"

"THE WAY, THE TRUTH, AND THE LIFE."

"Jesus saith, I am the way, the truth, and the life: no man cometh unto the Father, but by me."—JOHN xiv. 6.

NOTHING can be more important to sinners, than instruction in the person and work of Jesus Christ. Nothing can be more blessed for sinners than that Jesus Christ should give this instruction himself. Ministers preach Jesus Christ, but they may make mistakes, they are fallible men; Jesus Christ is the "faithful and true witness;" he is infallible; he knows all things; and, concerned as he is for our welfare, what could be more profitable to sinners than that he should teach them about himself? There are many things respecting Jesus Christ which the restless curiosity of man would pry into: as the nature of his eternal union with the Father; the mysteries of his incarnation; how his human soul could be distinct from, and yet subordinate to his Divine mind. These things he does not unveil; but he teaches us that which is of infinite moment to us as immortal and responsible creatures, namely, the way of salvation through himself: "I am the way, the truth, and the life."

"I am the way:"—"no man cometh unto the Father, but by me." Christ is then our way to God. He does not say, "I am *a* way," but "I am *the* way." There is but one way to God. Jesus Christ is that one way. Many ways lead from God: one only way conducts us to him. There are many diseases to which man is liable; there are many errors afloat in society: but health and truth are marked by unity. There are many ways to hell; there is but one way to heaven. "There is one God, and one mediator between God and men, the man Christ Jesus."

How mighty is the abyss between God and the creature, between a holy God and a sinner! an abyss which man, by his own folly and impiety, is daily making wider and deeper. Who but Jesus Christ could bridge over this mighty chasm? In tender mercy, he became our "mediator," or "daysman," laying his hand, as it were, upon the offended Father, and man his rebellious creature, and reconciling us to God in himself. By his incarnation, obedience, and sufferings, by his holy life and meritorious death, he has wrought our redemption. He has removed all obstacles to our return to God on God's part. The obedience which the law required, he has fulfilled. The penalty which justice exacted, as the right of the broken law, he has suffered, and in him "God can be just, and the justifier of him that believeth in Jesus." On our part the difficulties have been removed: the pride, vanity, worldliness, rebellion, and alienation of man's heart, all yield before the influence of the Holy Spirit, which Jesus has obtained as the Father's gift to man. Thus has Jesus effected a double reconciliation, the reconciliation of God to man, and of man to God. When a ship is going down off-shore, when she has dashed upon some hidden rock, and the billows are breaking over her with terrific fury, then a rope is thrown out from the shore, and laid hold of by the mariners, and fastened to the vessel. This line of communication is fastened at both ends, and, clinging to it, the weather-beaten crew are brought to the desired haven. The plan of salvation originated in the grace of God: Jesus came into the world "to seek and to save that which was lost;" and laying hold upon him, we are brought to God, to holiness, and to heaven.

"I am the way." How solemn is our Saviour's admonition, "Enter ye in at the strait gate: for wide is the gate, and broad is the way, that leadeth to destruction, and many there be which go in thereat: because strait is the gate, and narrow is the way, which leadeth unto life, and few there be that find it." "The whole world lieth in wickedness." Christ's people are a "little flock." "Many are called, but few are chosen." The prophet Isaiah thus describes the way: "An highway shall be there, and a way, and it shall be called the way of holiness; the unclean shall not pass over it; but it shall be for those: the wayfaring men, though fools, shall not err therein. No lion shall be there, nor any ravenous beast shall go up thereon; it shall not be found there: but the redeemed shall walk there. And the ransomed of the Lord shall return, and come to Zion with songs and everlasting joy upon their heads: they shall obtain joy and gladness, and sorrow and sighing shall flee away." There are many striking points in this passage. Of gospel times, it is predicted that there shall be a "highway"—a way plainly laid down and marked out. In the Scripture there are dark and difficult statements, but the way of salvation by Christ Jesus is clearly revealed; and the Holy Spirit is freely promised in answer to prayer. This way is a "way of holiness," it leads to a holy God, and a holy heaven. Whom Jesus saves, he sanctifies. "His mercy," says Bishop Reynolds, "is a holy mercy, which knows how to pardon sin, not to protect it. It is a sanctuary for the penitent, not for the presumptuous. The beam of the sun shining on fire doth discourage its burning: the shining of God's mercies on us should dishearten and extinguish lust in us. This is the use we should make of mercy. Say not, he is *my* God, therefore I may presume upon him; but, he is *mine*, therefore I must return unto him. Because he is God, I will fear to provoke him; and because he is *mine*, I will be afraid to forfeit him. He is so great, I must not dare to offend him: he is so precious, I must not venture to lose him." This is the law of Christ's kingdom—Without holiness no man shall see the Lord. It is added, "The unclean shall not pass over it," for vain is the profession of the gospel without the practice of its duties; "but it shall be for those," that is, if we adhere to our version, it shall be the happiness of those to walk in this way who are spoken of in the previous part of the chapter, and who are vitally interested in Jesus Christ, however ignorant they may be; "the wayfaring men, though fools, shall not err therein." In the margin, however, we read, "but he" (that is the Lord) "shall be with them." Bishop Lowth gives this beautiful translation of the verse:—

> " And a highway shall be there ;
> And it shall be the way of holiness ;
> No unclean person shall pass through it :
> But He himself shall be with them, walking in the way ;
> And the foolish shall not err therein."

The security of the way is set forth in the next verse, "No lion shall be there, nor any ravenous beast shall go up thereon; it shall not be found there." What have they to fear from temptation or conflict, if the Lord be with them "walking in the way?" "No weapon that is formed against thee shall prosper, and every tongue that shall rise against thee in judgment thou shalt condemn." All this high and distinguishing privilege implies the happiness of the way. "The ransomed of the Lord shall return" from their weary captivity under sin and Satan, and "they shall come to Zion with songs;" yea, "they shall sing in the ways of the Lord: for great is the glory of the Lord." Not only shall they obtain joy and gladness when they arrive at Zion, but they shall sing with unspeakable joy on their way thither; for wisdom's ways "are ways of pleasantness, and all her paths are peace." How blessed, then, must be the way of salvation! It is the way of holiness, liberty, security, and happiness, and terminates in everlasting glory.

The apostle, writing to the Hebrews, says, "Having therefore, brethren, boldness to enter into the holiest by the blood of Jesus, by a new and living way, which he hath consecrated for us, through the veil, that is to say, his flesh." The properties of this way are two. It is a *new* way, because, in contrast with the dispensation of the law, it was newly made, and belonged to the new covenant; it has also a perpetual freshness and power; it admits of no decay, believers find it ever new, and ever glorious. "It is a *living* way, in opposition to the way into the holiest, which was by *death:* nothing was done without the blood of sacrifices; and it is living, as to its efficacy; it hath a vital, spiritual efficacy in our access unto God: it leads to life, and effectually brings us thereto." *

Is Jesus Christ the way? Is he the one mediator? Let us come by him to God. Do we feel our ignorance? Let us say, "Teach me thy way, O Lord, and I will walk in thy truth: Oh knit my heart unto thee, that I may fear thy name." Do we need guidance? Let us plead the promise, "I

* Dr. Owen.

will instruct thee, and teach thee in the way which thou shalt go: I will guide thee with mine eye."

Is Jesus Christ the way? Let us persevere therein; one step will not take us to heaven. He only that endures to the end shall be saved. Every day will bring fresh exercise for grace; every day, therefore, should find us at the mercy-seat, drawing near to God by his dear Son.

Is Jesus Christ the way? Let us invite others to walk therein. Let us imitate the kindness of Moses to Hobab, and say to others, "We are journeying unto the place of which the Lord said, I will give it you: come thou with us, and we will do thee good: for the Lord hath spoken good concerning Israel." What millions are ignorant of Jesus, the way of pardon, peace, and holiness! Let us with joyful zeal tell them of this blessed way to God. What multitudes are there near our own doors, to whom Christ is still unknown! Let us endeavour to bring these to him.

I am the "truth." The ceremonies of the law were but shadows and types of "good things to come." Christ is the truth in whom all these shadows find their substance. The Epistle to the Hebrews is an inspired commentary on the Gospel according to Leviticus. For "what," says an old writer, "is the law, but the gospel predicted? and what is the gospel, but the law fulfilled?" The gospel is a key which unlocks the treasures of the law. The ancient Jews groaned under the weight of complicated and expensive ceremonies. We enjoy the riches of gospel light and consolation, laid up in those ceremonies. "The law is our schoolmaster to bring us to Christ." Not only is he the true manna, and the "spiritual Rock," but the tabernacle, its structure, ordinances, and priesthood, direct us to Christ the Truth. We wrong our own souls by studying these types so little. Take up the Bibles of many, even sincere Christians, and you will observe that the New Testament and Psalms have been carefully read; that the prophets have been but little read, and that Exodus and Leviticus have been scarcely opened. What was David's prayer? "Open thou mine eyes, that I may behold wondrous things out of thy law." In David's time, the Pentateuch was the only written voice of God to man, yet he speaks of wondrous things in the law, and he wrote a Psalm, consisting of 176 verses, to express his thankfulness for, and his admiration of a part of the sacred volume, which we Christians are too apt to neglect.

I am the "truth." "The testimony of Jesus is

the spirit of prophecy." How accurately have the prophecies of the Old Testament been fulfilled! Christ is the truth of each and of all of them. Christ is the "Seed of the woman;" the "Shiloh, to whom the nations will be gathered;" the "Branch from the root of Jesse," the "Ruler from Bethlehem," the "King, meek and lowly, riding upon an ass," the "Man of sorrows," and the "Sun of righteousness."

I am the "truth." In the midst of the false systems of religion in the world, Christ is the one Truth. Mohammedanism glories in its prophet: Christ is the true Prophet. Paganism is a lie: Christianity is truth. It may be asked, "There are many forms of Christianity; are all true?" We answer, All contain some portion of saving truth; but that which exhibits most of Christ, exhibits most of the truth. The more closely any teaching adheres to the word of God, and the more simply Christ is exalted, the more highly will God be honoured, and the more richly will the souls of men be blessed. We do not mean that the name of Christ is to occur in every sentence in a sermon, for there may be Christ's name, and not Christ's truth. But Christ, in all his work and offices, should be set forth. The love of Christ as our motive, and the law of

Christ as our rule; the atonement of Christ as our hope, and the example of Christ as our pattern; the all-sufficient merits of his Godhead, and the tender sympathy of his manhood; the grace which sways the heart to obey him, and the awful responsibility of rejecting him; the first coming of Christ, the centre of our confidence, and his second coming, the circumference of our hope; our absolute need and wretchedness without him, and our complete redemption and restoration through him — such are some of the main features of the truth of the gospel. Any system that hides or obscures these doctrines, however plausible its pretensions, is not to be regarded as a faithful exponent of the truth. Whatever differences of opinion may exist among serious Christians on matters of doctrine and church government, they are united in faith in the one Saviour. The Bible is their one standard of doctrine and duty; the Lord Jesus is the one foundation of their acceptance with God; the Holy Spirit is their one teacher, "dividing to every man severally as he will;" and heaven is their one eternal home.

"What is truth?" was the question of Pilate, but he did not wait for the reply. Jesus of Nazareth, the Truth, stood before him. The Roman governor was far too proud and worldly minded to seek instruction from the mysterious prisoner at the bar. The infidel and the scoffer reiterate the question, "What is truth?" and they endeavour to justify their neglect of the gospel by an appeal to the diversities of opinion among Christians. "Let them agree among themselves as to what is truth, and then we will condescend to listen to them." This, however, is a delusion, and often a cloak for sin. The love of sin is the root of infidelity. Let a man profess infidelity, and his conscience is not at peace. He may be noisy and merry with his companions; but he cannot, with all his efforts, divest himself of the sense of his individual responsibility: this tortures him when alone. There is a God, and reason coincides with conscience in the acknowledgment that God observes men's actions, and will judge them at the great day. There is that in man which is immortal; and there must therefore be some residence for the immortal spirit after death. There must be an eternity; and the man tremblingly asks, "What is truth?" If infidelity be sound and substantial, well; but if not, then where am I? what is my hope? what will become of me in a future state? what shall I answer to my Judge? Let such a man go to the Bible, and there he will find simple and majestic truth. A traveller who had professed infidel opinions was sailing to South America. The voyage was tedious, and he sought to beguile the time by reading. Among the few books which the ship afforded, was a copy of Rollin's "Arts and Sciences of the Ancients." There he met with some references to the Bible and to the fulfilment of its prophecies. He had not read the sacred volume for years. His curiosity about these prophecies led him to inquire for a Bible. He searched the ship through, and at length, at the bottom of a sailor's chest, one was discovered. He eagerly compared Rollin's references, and found them exactly correct. This induced him to read further. He had abundance of leisure, and the perusal became increasingly interesting. Gradually a serious impression fastened on his mind. At first, he rather tried to shake it off, and his associates on the voyage joked him about it. He could not explain it, and there was no one in the ship who could sympathize with his new feelings. He persevered in reading, and he found a happiness and rest, to which hitherto he had been a stranger. He no longer wished to shake off these convictions. Under the secret teaching of the Holy Ghost, he learned the fundamental doctrines of the gospel; and the first Sunday after his return to

England, he went to church, where, to his surprise and joy, he heard the very truths which he had worked out alone on shipboard, preached before the great congregation. This brought to his mind fresh evidence of the truth, and he "went on his way rejoicing." To the candid inquirer Christ says, "If any man will do his will, he shall know of the doctrine, whether it be of God, or whether I speak of myself."

I am the "life." What a beautiful completeness does this title give to the whole statement! For if there be a spiritual way to walk in, and a spiritual truth to apprehend, there must be spiritual life, or else neither the way nor the truth will profit us. How delightful, then, to hear Christ say, "I am the way, the truth, and the *life!*"

In Christ is life. Mental energy and spiritual life are his gift. How mysterious, and yet how powerful a principle is spiritual life! "The wind bloweth where it listeth, and thou hearest the sound thereof, but canst not tell whence it cometh, and whither it goeth: so is every one that is born of the Spirit." One soul is quickened suddenly, and with alarming convictions; another is led gradually and gently into the obedience of faith. The heart of the savage jailer is riven as by an earthquake, and in an agony of terror he cries out, "What must I do to be saved?" The heart of the devout Lydia is opened gently, like the first beginning of a summer day, or the passing away of a morning mist. It was real, and yet drew no notice. Happy Lydia! She went to the river-side, and returned home again the same woman outwardly, but inwardly how different! She went a stranger to Christ—she returned a sister beloved.

How various are the times for the commencement of this life! Some, like John the Baptist, are "filled with the Holy Ghost" from infancy. Others, as Samuel and Timothy, are called by Christ, and savingly instructed in the Scripture, in childhood. Some, like Josiah, are enabled to dedicate their youthful prime to God. Others, as Manasseh, are brought, after a long course of rebellion, to repentance. Some are converted in the midst of the pressing occupations of life, as Elisha and Matthew. We read of one who was forgiven and saved in the hour of death. One such case is recorded that none may despair; and only one, that none may presume.

The circumstances, also, of conversion vary greatly. The word of God is the instrument generally employed, but it is applied to the heart by different agencies. The lesson in the nursery; the sermon in the house of God; the conversation of a pious friend; the letter written for the birth-day; the Bible found in the knapsack, in the hour of loneliness, in a foreign land; the tract picked up on the wayside; the disappointment in business; the sudden death of a relative; or a season of prolonged sickness and retirement,—these are some of the channels through which Christ pours life into the soul. Amidst this diversity of operation, and variety in time and circumstances, the work is one and the same. In harmony, there is frequently the same air hidden under several variations. So in the spiritual dealings of Christ with men, there may be diversity and yet unity. Every case of conversion is marked by blessed fruits—repentance toward God, faith toward our Lord Jesus Christ, and love to man and zeal for God for Christ's sake. Conversion is a new creation—a passing from death to life, and from the power of Satan to God.

Christ is our "life." He nourishes the seed which he has planted. He who gives being, will also give increase. He who lays the foundation stone, will, according to his eternal purpose, carry on the building, and shall bring forth the head-stone thereof with shoutings, crying, "Grace, grace unto it." The promises are sure and faithful: "They go from strength to strength, every one of them in Zion appeareth before God." "The righteous also shall hold on his way, and he that hath clean hands shall be stronger and stronger." If conversion be a miracle of grace, the support and strength which the child of God receives from day to day is a continuation of the miracle. Neither the temptations of Satan, nor the allurements of the world, nor the corruptions of his own heart shall be permitted to prevail finally against the humble believer. Is it wonderful that the frail bark should outlive the raging tempest? No less wonderful are the victories of faith. Does the timid swallow, in her flight across the ocean towards a more genial climate, find that, in escaping from the monster bird of prey above her, she is in danger from the jaws of the devouring shark beneath her, so that on every side death threatens her? Yet is she sustained by the hand of Omnipotence, and carried forward by an invisible Protector. Even so, O Christian, "thy shoes shall be iron and brass; and as thy days, so shall thy strength be." Thine enemy is mighty, but thy Redeemer is mightier. In all things thou shalt be more than conqueror through him that hath loved thee. Look, then, unto Jesus, the "author and finisher of thy faith." Wait upon him, and he shall renew thy strength. Walk with him in lowly, self-renouncing dependence. Walk before him in the realization of his presence and love. Walk in him, rooted and built up in him. Expect nothing from thyself, everything from Jesus. Attempt nothing for self, but everything for him. And Christ, who has been thy way to God, and the truth to keep thee in the way, will be thy life to welcome and to crown thee at the end of the way.

"THE VINE."

" I am the true vine."—JOHN xv. 1.

"THE common people heard" Jesus Christ "gladly." Their "eyes were fastened upon him" while he spake to them, for he taught not only with power, and as "one having authority," but with great plainness of speech and illustration. He adapted his instruction to the capacities of men of ordinary life. His infinite knowledge would have enabled him to adorn and enforce his discourses with figures and emblems drawn from the secrets of creation, or the mysteries of his Father's being and attributes. But his teaching was not intended to win man's admiration, but to promote man's spiritual benefit. He drew his lessons, therefore, from familiar objects. A husbandman casting seed into the ground; the fisherman and his nets; the woman kneading dough, supplied him with a text and a similitude. Whether at home or abroad, everything with our Lord was a vehicle of instruction. A casual expression, an incidental occurrence, the season of the year, a particular place, the vicinity of a building, the features of the surrounding country, served to introduce matters of the greatest moment. He was, indeed, "a teacher sent from God;" never did an idle word fall from his gracious lips; in everything it was the study of his life to do all to the glory of his Father and for the salvation of man.

A tree is a common emblem in the Bible; the godly are spoken of as "trees of righteousness, the planting of the Lord, that he might be glorified;" and, in awful contrast, sinners are called "trees whose fruit withereth, without fruit, twice dead, plucked up by the roots." A particular tree is sometimes selected: "The righteous shall flourish like the palm-tree; he shall grow like a cedar in Lebanon." There can be no doubt that when our Lord pronounced the curse upon the barren fig-tree, it was a significant warning to the Jewish nation. The vine was as common in Palestine as the oak and the elm are with us; hence it could be no matter of surprise or difficulty to the apostles when our Lord, in his farewell discourse, said to them, "I am the true vine, and my Father is the husbandman."

Let us, then, meditate on this title which Jesus

has claimed for himself and his people, "I am the vine, ye are the branches."

"I am the vine." In outward appearance the vine is inferior to many trees. It is not as sturdy as the oak, nor as majestic as the cedar, nor as lofty as the palm. Look at the vine in early spring; it appears a dry, withered, sapless, lifeless, and leafless tree. Wait a few months; look again in autumn. What are those sounds of rejoicing? It is the joy of the vintage. The vines are covered with luxuriant foliage, and are adorned with rich purple fruit. The prophet thus describes the appearance of the Lord Jesus in this world:—"He shall grow up before him as a tender plant, and as a root out of a dry ground: he hath no form nor comeliness; and when we shall see him, there is no beauty that we should desire him;" and this is the testimony of the apostle, "that, though he was rich, yet for our sakes he became poor, that we through his poverty might be rich." Our Lord himself says, "The foxes have holes, and the birds of the air have nests; but the Son of man hath not where to lay his head." Think of the poverty of Jesus. He never possessed a habitation or an apartment he could call his own. He was born in another man's house, and this was a stable; and he was laid in a manger.

How soon was he driven an infant exile into Egypt! Widows ministered to him of their substance. Wearied with his journey, he sat on the well, and said to the woman, "Give me to drink." A fish furnished him with money to pay the temple tribute. One night he slept in a fishing-boat; another, he continued all night in prayer on a mountain. We read only once of his riding; and this was upon a borrowed ass, and a colt the foal of an ass. He partook of the last passover in a borrowed chamber; he was wrapped in linen not his own when taken down from the cross, and was buried in another man's garden, and another man's tomb. Who would have thought that this was the living Vine which should fill the face of the earth with fruit? When we think of the conversions on the day of Pentecost, and of the spread of Christianity from that day to this; when we contemplate the blessings, moral, social, and spiritual, which have everywhere followed the preaching of the gospel; when we think of the millions in the heavenly rest who have believed in Jesus, and who have triumphed through him; when we cast our eye over the world, upon multitudes of every nation, kindred, people, and tongue, who, sprinkled like gems among all denominations, are his militant church on earth, who rest upon him, love him, and glorify him,—then we understand why he has compared himself to a vine, a tree so full of life, joy, and fruitfulness.

The foliage of the vine affords delightful shade. We read in the Scripture of persons sitting under the vine and under the fig-tree. In reference to another tree, the bride, the church says of her Beloved, "I sat down under his shadow with great delight, and his fruit was sweet to my taste." Christ affords the shadow of protection and refreshment to his people. He defends them in the hour of temptation and danger. He shelters them from the wrath of God, the curse of the broken law, and the accusations of an awakened and upbraiding conscience. This shadow is represented under a fourfold emblem: first, that of a tree, as we have just stated; second, that of a cloud, as in Isaiah xxv. 5; third, that of a rock, "a great rock in a weary land;" and fourth, that of a tabernacle: "There shall be a tabernacle for a shadow in the daytime from the heat." The shadow of a tree under which we sit down is delightful; but it is limited to a small distance, and the solar rays frequently pierce through the boughs. The shadow of a cloud in harvest is grateful, but transient. The shadow of a great rock is dense and cool: but it befriends not on every side, and covers little from the vertical rays. The shadow of a tabernacle is the most complete and inviting. All these have some truth in their application to Christ; but none do justice to him. He is what they imply, and infinitely more, because he is Divine. How beautiful, then, and how just, is this emblem of the true Vine! The fruit, however, must be tasted, and the shade experienced to be appreciated. We must come to Christ, and taste how gracious he is, and how complete is the peace and protection which he bestows, if we desire personally to realize these inestimable blessings. This emblem teaches us as much by contrast as by comparison. A vine is not always green; it will not always bear; and it bears only one kind of fruit. Christ ever liveth; he is unchangeably the same, "yesterday, to-day, and for ever." He has all grace in himself, and he bestows it upon his needy suppliants at all times and under all circumstances. He is the Tree of life that bears "twelve manner of fruits." All that the soul can require is laid up in him, and out of his fulness may we receive, and "grace for grace." The fruit and shade of the vine are only temporal and for the body: Christ is a Saviour for the soul and for eternity. The poor cannot obtain wine; but poverty excludes none from the wine of the gospel. Here "the rich and the poor meet together." The fruit of the vine, if taken too largely, will injure the partaker; but there is no danger here; while we are forbidden to be "drunk with wine, wherein is excess," we are commanded to be "filled with the Spirit."

"Ye are the branches." This is the title which the Lord Jesus gives to his disciples, and it implies their union to him. This union may be external and scarcely apparent, or internal and real. We are outwardly united to Christ when we are admitted into his visible church, when we attend the ordinances of the sanctuary, and are called Christians. Many are thus outwardly united to Christ while their hearts are given to the world. Occasionally, nay, perhaps regularly, they attend the means of grace, but, alas, this is the only homage which they pay to religion. Even on the Sabbath, their conversation is of the world, worldly; and through the week they are wholly engrossed with the cares, and pleasures, and riches of this life. To such as these Christ refers when he says, "Every branch in me that beareth not fruit he taketh away." It is their high and awful privilege that they are outwardly united to Christ: it is their condemnation that with all their profession they bear no fruit of faith, love, and holy obedience; and it will be their tremendous doom to be "taken away" and "cast into outer darkness," where "there shall be weeping and gnashing of teeth."

There are those who are inwardly and truly united to Jesus, and these are the true church, and the little flock to whom it is the Father's good pleasure to give the kingdom. Christ is the true Vine, and these are fruit-bearing branches. How is this union produced? What is its nature? What are its blessed results? How is this vine-slip to be made partaker of the life and fatness of the true vine? By creating the closest connection possible. You engraft it. You take this leafless rod, perhaps severed from a wild vine, and you insert it in the quick vine-stock, and speedily the graft has taken. Fibre by fibre, and vein by vein, the slip clings and coheres, till the life of the tree is the life of this adopted branch, and the graft buds, and blossoms, and matures its clusters from the flowing juices of the vine.* Jesus has life in himself, and having completed the work given him to do, he rests in his Father's bosom, and is most blessed for evermore. But here is a dead and sapless soul; here is a spirit to which holy joy is a stranger, and to which

* "The Vine." Nisbet's Series of Tracts.

God is still unknown as a reconciled God and a loving Father. How is this dead and dreary soul to be made partaker of Christ's life and joy? It must be separated from the wild tree of nature, and it must be brought into the closest connection with Jesus Christ, the living tree of grace. It is the husbandman who effects the graft. Conversion is an instance of Divine interposition. Left to itself, the barren branch would have remained in the wild tree, and would have yielded no profitable fruit. But the husbandman cut it off the wild vine, and grafted it into the true vine. Our heavenly Father, by the power of the Holy Spirit upon his word, and his providential dealings, separates the soul from worldly dependence, tastes, and pleasures, and graciously leads it by faith to cling to Jesus. Life flows from this true vine into the soul of the humble penitent. This life is soon evidenced by growth and fruitfulness.

Though the union of the believer with Christ be mysterious, it is real, close, intimate, and endearing. Any injury inflicted upon his people, Christ regards as done to himself: "Saul, Saul, why persecutest thou me?" "He that toucheth you toucheth the apple of his eye." And any kindness shown to them, he will crown with an abundant recompense: "Whosoever shall give to drink unto one of these little ones a cup of cold water only in the name of a disciple, verily I say unto you, he shall in no wise lose his reward." "Inasmuch as ye have done it unto one of the least of these my brethren, ye have done it unto me." On the other hand, the glory of Christ is dear to the Christian. It is his highest joy to see the kingdom of Christ advanced, and his greatest grief to see Christ dishonoured or rejected: "Rivers of waters run down mine eyes, because men keep not thy law." As the same sap pervades the vine and the branches, so the same mind is in his people which was also in Christ Jesus; for "he that is joined to the Lord is one spirit." There is confidence in this union. How wonderful to hear the Lord say, "Shall I hide from Abraham that thing which I do?" and how unfathomable the condescension, that he should impart his counsels to sinful worms of the dust! "The secret of the Lord is with them that fear him." "To you it is given to know the mysteries of the kingdom of heaven." It may be said, these were his apostles, and they were honoured with peculiar confidence: it cannot be so in our day. We answer, that in measure it is the same now. Christ speaks to the souls of his people now as distinctly and as personally as when 1800 years ago he held communion with the apostles face to face, as "a man speaketh to his friend." His word dwells in them richly in all wisdom, and many a dark and frowning providence he explains to them by the secret whispers of his love. So that it is their happiness "to lie passive in his hands, and know no will but his." This experience of Christ's love increases confidence in him. What a blessed welcome did the penitent receive when with trembling fears he cast himself at the foot of the cross! That welcome has bound his heart to Christ ever since. Every day has witnessed his believing access to the same cross, and to the fountain of all cleansing efficacy; and every fresh welcome inflames his love to the Saviour more and more. He knows and is sure that Christ is his Saviour and his Friend; he has learned to "trust in him at all times, and to pour out his heart before him;" yea, to "come boldly unto the throne of grace, that he may obtain mercy, and find grace to help in time of need." There is great consolation in this union with Christ. Where a union is formed between persons, and one is superior to the other in wisdom and power, the weaker party looks up to the superior with reverence and dependence. Immeasurable indeed is the disparity between the Divine Saviour and the miserable sinner. Hence the believer hangs upon Jesus for all things. He trusts in Christ for wisdom, righteousness, sanctification, and redemption. He knows that he can do nothing of himself, and, therefore, he looks to Christ in every duty, trial, and emergency. But though the branches depend on the parent stock for all their life, beauty, and fruitfulness, yet the branches are the glory of the vine. Christians are the glory of Christ. He sustains them, and they glorify him. From him is their fruit found as its source, but they bear the fruit to the "praise and glory of God." They receive from Christ, and work for him. They live in the Spirit and they walk in the Spirit. And the "fruit of the Spirit is love, joy, peace, long-suffering, gentleness, goodness, faith, meekness, temperance."

Union with Christ is characterized by progressive sanctification. Every fruitful branch is purged. "The husbandman purgeth it, that it may bring forth more fruit." It is the propensity of even fruitful branches to wanton into excessive foliage. But besides spoiling the appearance of the vine, the sap spent on the leaves is taken from the grapes, and the excessive shade keeps out the sun. The husbandman prunes these shoots and suckers away; and while he makes the branch more sightly, he lets the sunbeams freely in, and makes the clusters richer. So it is with Christians. In prosperity, when all goes well with them, they are apt to indulge in pride and luxury. They grow selfish, and study their own ease. They seek great things for themselves. And the watchful husbandman, consulting his own glory in the fruitfulness of the vine, comes with the pruning-knife of some afflictive providence and removes the verdant shoots. Not to hurt, but to benefit the tree does the husbandman handle the pruning-knife. In deep dejection of spirit, Mr. Cecil was pacing to and fro in the Botanic Garden at Oxford, when he observed a fine specimen of the pomegranate almost cut through the stem. On asking the gardener the reason, he received an answer which explained the wounds of his own bleeding spirit,—"Sir, this tree used to shoot so strong that it bore nothing but leaves. I was, therefore, obliged to cut it in this manner, and when it was almost cut through, then it began to bear plenty of fruit." Ye suffering members of Christ, be thankful for every sorrow which weakens sin or strengthens grace. Though it should be a cut to the heart, be thankful for every sin and idol shorn away; for whatever makes your conscience more tender and your character more consistent.

Another privilege flowing from union with Christ, is success in prayer. "If ye abide in me, and my words abide in you, ye shall ask what ye will, and it shall be done unto you." To abide in Christ is to maintain communion with him, not only at stated seasons, not only in secret, family, and public worship, but in our daily walk and conversation. To abide in Christ is to have the heart constantly going forth to him in meditation on his person, offices, and work; to have the mental eye ever fixed upon him in grateful, loving, holy adoration and praise. To abide in Christ is to have our wills and affections so subdued to the "obedience of faith," that the one object and desire of our hearts and lives is to imitate his example, and to keep his commandments. To quicken and maintain and direct this blessed union with Christ, it is necessary that his words should abide in us. It is the application of the word of God with power to the judgment and conscience, that imparts the true vine nature to the branches. "Ye are clean," that is, pure and genuine, "through the word which I have spoken unto you." This word abides in their hearts from day to day. Its precepts and promises; its encouragements and warnings; its moral lessons and evangelical motives; its examples of holiness and its anticipations of exalted happiness—these are treasured up in the hearts of Christians, and exercise a transforming influence over them, so that they grow up into Christ in all things.

Abiding in Christ, and Christ's word abiding in them, believers know and love and are conformed to the will of Christ. Thus they have a spiritual perception of that which will please their Lord and Saviour. Here is the secret of their strength in prayer. The apostle John teaches us that "this is the confidence that we have in him, that if we ask anything according to his will, he heareth us." It is the privilege of believers, that they have access to God in Christ Jesus. Their prayers are the communings of children with a Father. Temporal things they are well content to leave to his disposal, and spiritual blessings they may ask with holy boldness, because they know that the will of God is their sanctification. The answers to prayer which they daily receive, and which they love to register in their affectionate remembrance, are testimonies to their interest in Christ, and their adoption into the family of God. It is their duty to have their hearts in that state and frame, that they shall instantly recognize the answer to their supplications, the response from the mercy-seat in heaven to the telegraphic communications dispatched from the spiritual worshippers on earth.

We have thus briefly considered the nature and efficacy of union* with Christ. Let us inquire whether we are living branches in him the true Vine. "They are not all Israel, which are of Israel." It is one thing to be a Christian in name, and another to be a Christian in deed. Have we been taught our sinfulness and danger by the Holy Spirit? Have we been enabled by grace to believe in Christ? Is he all our salvation and all our desire? Do we maintain communion with him? Do we esteem the words of his mouth more than our necessary food? Do we bear fruit to the glory of

---

* This subject is treated in a devout and practical manner in a book called "Thoughts on Union with Christ;" by Sosthenes.

his name? Is our conscience tender, our eye single, our demeanour serious and holy? Are we "epistles of Christ, known and read of all men?" "And now, little children, abide in him; that, when he shall appear, we may have confidence, and not be ashamed before him at his coming."

"THE MORNING STAR."

"I am the root and the offspring of David, and the bright and morning star."—REV. xxii. 16.

WE have now meditated upon the glorious titles which our blessed Lord has assumed to himself in the New Testament. We have observed that some of these are personal, and that others are pictorial titles. When he calls himself, "I Am;" "Alpha and Omega;" "Jesus;" "Christ;" "The Son of God," and "The Son of man," it is plain that these are personal titles in which he sets forth what he is in himself. When our Lord compares himself to the "manna;" a "shepherd;" a "door;" a "way," and a "vine," it is equally plain that these emblems he employs as pictorial representations of the offices that he bears to his redeemed people. The verse at the head of this chapter contains the last of these self-assumed titles in the Holy Scriptures, and combines in striking and sublime language that which is personal with that which is pictorial. "I am the root and the offspring of David;" here is the august and mysterious person of Christ: "I am the bright and morning Star;" here is an appropriate and consolatory emblem of his work and office. An especial blessing is pronounced upon the devout and intelligent perusal of the book of Revelation. "Blessed is he that readeth, and they that hear the words of this prophecy, and keep those things which are written therein: for the time is at hand." The prophecies of this book embrace the history of the church of Christ from his ascension to his coming again. Some of these prophecies were addressed to the beloved disciple by the ministry of an angel, and others by the Lord himself. But in the titles, which will form the subject of this our concluding chapter, he sets his seal to, and authenticates the whole book: "I Jesus have sent mine angel to testify unto you these things in the churches: I am the root and the offspring of David, and the bright and morning Star."

The Lord Jesus thus describes his personal character: "I am the root and the offspring of David." That he was according to the flesh, and in fulfilment of ancient prediction, "the offspring of David" is proved by the two genealogies given by Matthew and Luke, which trace his line of ancestry on his mother's and on his reputed father's side. In the wonder-working providence of God, Joseph repaired from Nazareth to Bethlehem to enrol his name in the register of that town, "because he was of the house and lineage of David." In doing this, Joseph simply obeyed the decree of Cæsar Augustus "that all the world should be taxed," that a census might be taken of the millions which composed his mighty empire. Mary, the espoused wife of Joseph, accompanied him—a fatiguing journey of more than sixty miles. Whilst at Bethlehem, she was delivered of her firstborn son; and the infant Saviour of the world was "laid in a manger, because there was no room for them in the inn." Thus singularly was it brought about, that Jesus was born at Bethlehem, and that his name and descent from David were publicly registered in that town. Christ was also the "root" of David. This he could only be in his Divine nature. The union of the two natures in one person is the only explanation of the paradox, "I am the root and the offspring of David." This the Pharisees could not solve: "What think ye of Christ?" was our Lord's question to them, the last question of his public ministry, "whose son is he? They say unto him, The Son of David. He saith unto them, How then doth David in spirit call him Lord? saying, The Lord said unto my Lord, Sit thou on my right hand, till I make thine enemies thy footstool. If David then call him Lord, how is he his son? And no man was able to answer him a word, neither durst any man from that day forth ask him any more questions."

Neither can the Unitarian explain this difficulty. For if Jesus Christ be only a man, if he be simply the offspring of David, how can he be the root of David? Christ was born one thousand years after David; but the root of David must be before David. If Christ then be only a man, how can he be the root of a very distant ancestor? No man that receives the New Testament can deny that, according to the flesh, Christ was the Son of David, and was born at Bethlehem. If he be David's Lord and David's root, then he must have existed long before he was "born of a pure virgin." The pre-existence of Christ necessarily implies his Deity. And if, instead of appealing to human reason, we go to the Scriptures, we shall find that the same passages which teach his humanity, also prove his Deity. Paul, speaking of the exalted privileges of the Jewish people, says, that of them "concerning the flesh Christ came," and he adds, "who is over all,

God blessed for ever. Amen." To quote only one more reference: "Behold," saith the prophet Isaiah, "a virgin shall conceive, and bear a son, and shall call his name Immanuel." Matthew has given us the inspired application of this prediction, and the interpretation of the name "Emmanuel, which is, God with us." In our present imperfect state we cannot fathom the mystery of the person of Christ. We are a mystery to ourselves. We cannot explain how the reasonable soul and flesh is one man: is it any matter of surprise that we cannot unravel the amazing mystery that "God and man is one Christ?" Let us receive the testimony of the word of truth with reverence and humility. Let us listen when God speaks, and believe and wait when he is silent. We have a Divine Saviour; let us build all our hope of eternal happiness upon him. We need, in the daily trials of life, a sympathizing Brother and Friend. Let us go to Jesus, who "was in all points tempted like as we are, yet without sin." He will not break the bruised reed, nor quench the smoking flax: he shall bring forth judgment unto truth. Let us adore and bless God for the revelation of so complete and glorious a Redeemer, who is so able and so willing to save, and who is "the root and the offspring of David."

We must, however, proceed to meditate on Jesus as "the bright and morning Star." This is no disparagement to him who is called the Sun. We have frequently observed that no emblem can do justice to him. The one Saviour is called the "Dayspring," the "Day Star," the "Light of the world," and the "Sun of righteousness."

The word star is used symbolically and for different purposes in the Bible. It is used to describe the angels of heaven, as in Job: "The morning stars sang together, and all the sons of God shouted for joy." By a star is meant a ruler, or a conqueror, as in the celebrated prophecy of Balaam, "I shall see him, but not now; I shall behold him, but not nigh: there shall come a star out of Jacob, and a sceptre shall rise out of Israel, and shall smite the corners of Moab, and destroy all the children of Sheth." The king of Babylon, in his pride, called himself the morning star; but his pride brought him low, for the morning star of Babylon was a fallen star. "How art thou fallen from heaven, O Lucifer, son of the morning!" Pastors or ministers of the gospel, who ought to shine like stars in respect of the brightness and purity of their lives and doctrine, are also called stars in Rev. i. 20, where they are said to be in Christ's hand, located and removed by him according to his ever wise and watchful providence. Again, wicked professors are called "wandering stars, to whom is reserved the blackness of darkness for ever."

Jesus Christ calls himself the "bright and morning Star." Of all the stars which bespangle the vault of heaven, the morning star* is the most luminous and beautiful. In all things Christ has the pre-eminence. He is fairer than the angels of God; fairer than the children of men: he is "the chiefest among ten thousand, and altogether lovely."

When other stars pale their radiance, the morning star shines forth. When prophecy had been silent four centuries, the great Prophet of the church appeared. When reason, unassisted by revelation, had failed in four thousand years to discover man's chief end, and his real happiness, then the true Light enlightened the world.

The bright and morning star is the harbinger of the day. It is principally in this reference that we are to understand the emblem which the Lord Jesus has assumed to himself. The aged Zacharias, in his prophetic song, extols "the tender mercy of our God; whereby the dayspring from on high hath visited us, to give light to them that sit in darkness

* The planet Venus is usually so called.

and in the shadow of death, to guide our feet into the way of peace." When the angels announced the birth of Christ to the shepherds, in the glowing anthem, "Glory to God in the highest, and on earth peace, good-will toward men;" when Christ, by his obedient life and atoning death, wrought out our redemption; when he rose from the dead and brought "life and immortality to light," and opened the kingdom of heaven to all believers; and when he stood upon Mount Olivet, and blessed his disciples, and gave them that wondrous commission, "Go ye into all the world, and preach the gospel to every creature,"—in all these events, we behold the Morning Star ushering in the noon-tide splendour. "When the morn is nearest, the night is drearest." The first two chapters of the Epistle to the Romans testify to the moral and spiritual darkness both of Jews and heathen. When truth had fallen in Jerusalem, and virtue starved at Rome; when the eye of Greece was almost darkened, and Egypt, once the nursery of letters, and the mistress of nations, had dwindled into a Roman province; then the Star of Bethlehem arose; truth again flourished upon the earth, and righteousness looked down from heaven. The morning star gives but a faint idea of the brightness of the noonday. The success of

Christ's ministry, and of the labours of his early followers, gave but a slender presage of the triumphs which Christianity should win from age to age. Who can number the rays of light which stream from the sun in his full-orbed glory? And what human arithmetic can calculate the moral, social, political, intellectual, and spiritual blessings which have accompanied the gospel of the Lord Jesus? "Truly the light is sweet, and a pleasant thing it is for the eyes to behold the sun;" but the light of Christianity and the truth of Jesus have conferred blessings upon us, which the heart of man cannot conceive, or his tongue describe.

Peter teaches us that "we have a more sure word of prophecy; whereunto ye do well that ye take heed, as unto a light that shineth in a dark place, until the day dawn, and the day-star arise in your hearts." Christ is this "day-star." Dark indeed, as a gloomy sepulchre, is the heart of man. Naturally, sin and death reign there with undisputed sway. When grace enters, the "day-star" arises. The sinner is taught by the Holy Spirit the exceeding sinfulness of sin; left to himself, he might despair of any effectual remedy, for he has no merit to atone for past transgressions, and no strength adequately to fulfil present duty, nor to vanquish present temptation: no hope, therefore, in himself of acceptance with God. What shall the trembling sinner do? The grace which has taught him his sinfulness, leads him to the cross. There he beholds "the Lamb of God, which taketh away the sin of the world." Hope is kindled in his breast; the "day-star" indeed arises; and the thrilling welcome which he receives from the Saviour inspires him with a humble confidence, that the grace which has begun will also perfect the happy work wrought in him, and that his path shall be like "the shining light, that shineth more and more unto the perfect day."

There is a day which Christians delight to anticipate, namely, the day of Christ's glorious reign upon our earth; of this day, the bright and morning Star is the harbinger. We believe that our lot is cast in very solemn times, and that our feet press upon the margin of the appearing of the Son of man. The prophet Zechariah, speaking of the period when Christ shall come, says that, "In that day the light shall not be clear, nor dark: but it shall be one day which shall be known to the Lord, not day, nor night: but it shall come to pass, that at evening time it shall be light." When we take a survey of the religious state of mankind, we behold vast multitudes who are still destitute of the true light, "without hope, and without God in the world." But the darkness which broods over millions, though intense, is not supreme. The pure gospel is widely proclaimed; the word of truth is largely circulated; Jesus has an innumerable host of faithful witnesses; and we rejoice in the belief, that never were greater exertions made than in the present day to speed the course of the gospel all the world over. There are signs of the times, to which we can with difficulty shut our eyes. How remarkable are the words of the ancient seer, containing a Divine photograph, as it were, of the very days in which we ourselves now live: "Many shall run to and fro, and knowledge shall be increased!" A living writer well remarks, that "the means of intercourse were never so abundant as in the present age. It is an age marked above all others for multiplying the means of rapid communication. All the efforts of mankind for promoting intercourse in the way of roads, and other communications from place to place, from the beginning of the world till the present time, are not nearly so great as the efforts which have been made, and the progress which has been attained during the last fifty years. What an illustration is this fact of the prophecy to which we have referred, and which was given to Daniel by the Son of man twenty-four hundred years ago!

But it is not merely that the *means* of intercourse have been very greatly increased: the *motives* for that intercourse have been increased, have completely changed the whole character of the age in which we live. Steamboats and railroads, electric telegraphs, submarine telegraphs, new lines of steamers, surpassing all the triumphs of science and art in former ages in size and swiftness—these are the subjects which are constantly uppermost in the thoughts of men. What do we witness at the present hour? These great efforts, all tending to promote more rapid communication between the farthest West and the extremest East, struggling, as it were, into birth. Supposing these plans completed, we shall witness such a spectacle as this earth has never witnessed before. We shall see the grasp of science taking hold of nearly the whole circumference of the globe, so that in a few minutes a message may be transmitted from the farthest East to California in the farthest West. No wonder, then, that such a signal feature of God's providence should be made the subject of prophecy in olden times, or that He who sees the end from the beginning should in these few words have stamped the very image of the times in which we live: "Many shall run to and fro, and knowledge shall be increased."

But the sign which we regard with the greatest interest, as the bright and morning star, the harbinger of the day of Christ's glory, is the propagation of the gospel among Jews and heathen. Fifty years ago scarcely any interest was taken in Zion; there were few who mourned over her desolations, and who prayed that her time of favour might come. Fifty years ago, but few missionaries were sent to the heathen. Now what a different state of things do we behold. Look at that great and glorious institution, the British and Foreign Bible Society. Fifty years ago the Scriptures went forth from the press through the world at the rate of 2000 copies per week; now the presses of the Bible Society alone send forth the word of God at the rate of 13,000 copies per day. Four hundred years ago, it occupied a year to transcribe a copy of the Holy Scriptures, and a fortune was required for its purchase; now, through the immense improvements in printing, by cylinder steam-presses, a whole Bible is printed in one minute, and is sold for twenty-five cents. Are we not reminded by this mighty extension of the truth of the Saviour's words, "The gospel shall be preached as a witness among all nations, and then shall the end come?" Contemplate, Christians, the bright and shining pledge of your Lord's return. "Lift up your heads with joy, for your redemption draweth nigh." "Now is your salvation nearer than when ye believed." "Yet a little while, and He that shall come will come, and will not tarry." "The Redeemer shall come to Zion," and the widowed land of Judah shall welcome her everlasting Bridegroom. The air which was once rent with the cry, "Crucify him, crucify him," shall resound with joyful acclamations, "Hosanna, Hosanna to the Son of David: blessed is he that cometh in the name of the Lord." The spirit of grace and of supplications shall be poured forth, and the house of David and the inhabitants of Jerusalem shall look upon Him whom they have pierced, and mourn over centuries of unbelief and hardness of heart. The glory of the Lord shall rise upon Zion, and the Gentiles shall come to her light, and kings to the brightness of her rising. The earth shall be filled with the knowledge of the glory of the Lord, as the waters cover the sea.

Seeing then that we look for such things, "what manner of persons ought we to be in all holy conversation and godliness!" Let us set the Lord Jesus constantly before us. Let us imitate him. Let us shine as lights in the world, and let us anticipate with joy the blessed period which is hastening on, when "they that be wise shall shine as the brightness of the firmament; and they that turn many to righteousness as the stars for ever and ever."

www.ingramcontent.com/pod-product-compliance
Lightning Source LLC
LaVergne TN
LVHW010255110826
845151LV00004B/1483

* 9 7 8 1 4 2 5 5 2 2 4 1 4 *